To Pat —

Memories of the past pass thru my mind all the time — the good times and the others we shared — I hope we can all be together soon — what a great visit! Certainly hope you enjoy this —

Bob

Sufferin' Springs Valley

SUFFERIN' SPRINGS VALLEY

Early Southeast Arizona As I Lived It

by Bob Bliss

*T*his book is affectionately dedicated to
my mother and father, both gone now.
These two wonderful people epitomized the
pioneer spirit of early Arizonans. They
were Christian people whose main purpose in
life was to serve their fellowman and their
family. They were my inspiration. Whoever
their lives touched were the better for having
had them in their midst.

Contents

Foreword

I'VE KNOWN BOB BLISS since we both were tooting trumpets in the Glendale Grammar School band. He had an unruly shock of blond hair that stood up as though electrified, and he wore a perpetual expression of wide-eyed amazement.

The reason for that expression eventually became evident to me. Bob appeared amazed at the world because he really was. And he has been fascinated with life ever since — intrigued by life's complexity, thrilled by the world's beauty, and captivated by the personalities of humankind.

Everything interested Bob. From athletics to music, from farming to mathematics, from politics to machinery, his quick mind turned with fascinated inquiry.

When he left Glendale, he enrolled in high school at Willcox. He savored all that life had to offer. Bliss was a three-sport varsity athlete, a dance band trumpeter, a vocalist of ability, a student of farming, and an extrovert who made it a point to know everybody for miles around.

Apparently he was a good listener, too, and one who remembered most of what he heard. This collection of stories about Willcox and Sulphur Springs Valley will attest to that.

When Bliss entered the University of Arizona in 1941, he enrolled in the pre-law program. He had the brains, the tenacity, and the gift of gab to become a good lawyer, too, but things didn't work out that way. Shortly after Pearl Harbor, he joined the Navy.

As a landing control officer on the aircraft carrier Wake Island, Bliss survived seven major naval engagements and visited five continents. Peleliu, Lingayen Gulf, Leyte, Iwo Jima, Okinawa, the Battle of the Atlantic, and many other battles are part of his wartime memories.

When he returned to the University of Arizona in 1946, he majored in political science. But his first job after graduation was with the U.S. Geological Survey, and he discovered he liked mathematical calculation, the challenge of civil engineering, and life in the outdoors.

Bliss has been involved in technical pursuits ever since: with Kennecott Copper Corporation in New Mexico, with North American Aviation and KAR Products in Oklahoma, with firms in Arizona and Texas, and, since 1974, as president of his own heavy equipment parts firm in Phoenix.

Foreword

He has never lost his fascination with people, nor his ability to communicate in writing or from a podium. He has been wanting to write this book about his youth in Willcox for decades, and now he has done it.

It's an authentic book because he lived most of it and remembered the rest from the tales of the remarkable people he grew up with.

The world and its endless variety of people still amaze Bob Bliss. For a writer, that's a mighty important ingredient.

Dean Smith, Director,
Publications
Arizona State University.

Preface

MANY TIMES I have written this book — in the small hours of the morning in the dark, along some highway, or just sitting in my chair, daydreaming. I guess everyone at one time or another dreams of writing the Great American Novel, but they just never do it. Finally, because of the great love of a certain lady and the realization that I'm not getting any younger, I decided I had better get on with it.

For those who dream of the one great book they will write someday, it is always about their hometown and their days growing up there — and this book is no different, except in a very special way. Most of these kinds of books are written about hometowns in the East, the New England states, or the South; few, if any, are about the Southwest. And the Southwest that I knew was young, raw-boned, and still in the process of making history. My hometown is in the very southeast of Arizona, which tells you something right there, because even today many people in other parts of the country feel we are still not as civilized as could be expected. And this area of southeastern Arizona is in the heart of probably the most historical part of these United States. This was the scene of the Coronado trek in search of the Lost Gold Cities of Cibola, the area traversed and lived in by Cochise and Geronimo and their people, the scene of the gunfighters Doc Holliday, Wyatt Earp, Johnny Ringo, and others. It was the "promised land" for many people who came to make their fortunes in the gold and silver mines and the towns that now lie in ruin and desolation — mute evidence of dreams, lost dreams. This area was the setting for just plain people making a living, who soon disappeared as the mines played out. And the beautiful valley surrounded by mountains was home to the cattleman, as it still is today.

In particular, however, this book is about the little town of Willcox, right in the heart of the valley. This is about my growing up there and the people and events that shaped my life. It was a wonderful time, filled with mostly the good things of life. This book is about my family and especially my mother and father, the two most beautiful people who ever lived. They're gone now, and it's hard to realize sometimes that they've been gone this long. One evening, not so long ago, in the spring of the year, I was driving from Fort Grant, north of Willcox, when I just had to stop the car and step out into the darkening evening. The stars were coming out brightly and starkly against the sky and the high mountains on all sides of me were dark and the air was still, and all that could be heard was the bawling of a cow off in the distance and the far-distant sound of an irrigation pump. I leaned against the car and felt that my folks were there with me. I felt their presence and the presence of all the people who had lived in this valley and had looked up at skies just like this; and I knew that I would have to write all this down someday, because of these people who had gone before. One has to feel close to his Maker at a time like this because of the feeling of the infinite time of the valley, the mountains, the stars, and the people. In fact, this experience moved me to write about it to my old Sunday School class back in Tulsa. As I stepped back into the car, I looked off into the distance at the lights of faraway farmhouses and ranches and even of Willcox, and I thought of my dad and mother and what their contribution to this world had been and whether I could ever live up to anything like it.

Another motivation in my writing this book is to try to prove a point in this day and age. Nowadays, many people do not feel any allegiance to the past, nor do they feel they owe anything to those who have gone on before. I hope to show in this book that I, and the young people of my time in Willcox, owed everything to those who had gone on before, just as the young people of Willcox and the valley now owe the same debts.

It is always this way. Someone had to pioneer this valley, settle it, develop it, civilize it, and bring it to the point that it is today. I can hear some of the young people say, "But look at all of the problems we are faced with, and we can't get help from those who went before." But I hope to say to them that the pioneers had just as many problems, and I am sure that they solved them by using some of the age-old truths of yesteryear and the experience of those who went before. This is also true in the world outside the valley.

With regard to the people and incidents related in this book, I am going to use real names or leave them out as the situation requires, and I will try to keep the incidents in their proper perspective. I once had a history professor at the University of Arizona who was quite an expert on Southwestern history, and he said that one thing the people of this area are guilty of is that their adventures grow a bit in stature from the doing to the telling. In other words, exaggeration becomes truth pretty darn quick as the tale gets told over and over. Now, I hope I won't be guilty of this, but let's face it, I'm getting up in years, and some of the things that happened to me in the thirties and forties may have changed a little in the remembering. But I think I have most of my facts straight. I feel that I have to say this because I am sure there are some of my contemporaries who may feel differently about some of the events about to be told. With regard

Map of Sulphur Springs Valley

to the people in this book, I am sure that most will recognize themselves, and I hope that I won't tread on any toes, because this is certainly not my intention.

This will certainly not be a contemporary book, and if the reader is looking for "way-out" adventure or sex, he or she is going to be very disappointed. Now, I'm not going to say that the people of the valley didn't think about the opposite sex or some of the other "pleasures" of life that have become a way of life today, because you are going to read about some goings-on that touch on these, and the valley has grown in population and not all of these people are immigrants. So, the people there knew about procreation.

As for the title of the book, I think it needs an explanation. If you look at the map of southeastern Arizona and find the little dot that denotes Willcox, you will also notice that the area around Willcox is a large valley set between the Dos Cabezas mountains, the Grahams, the Galiuros, and a part of the Chiricahuas on the north, the main part of the Chiricahuas and the Swisshelms on the east, a mountain range in northern Mexico on the south, and the Dragoons, Winchesters, and part of the Mules on the west. This is the Sulphur Springs Valley, deriving its name from dried-up springs near three small mountains known as the Three Sisters in the middle of the valley. These springs have quite a history. It was here that Wyatt Earp told the town of Tombstone that he left the body of Curly Bill Brocius, the infamous outlaw, after Earp had killed him in a gun battle. Brocius's body was never found. There are many stories about these old springs — most, I suspect, not to be known in fact. Anyway, as time progressed, a number of people came out of Texas, Kansas, New Mexico, and other areas to grub out a sometimes meager living on dry-land farms in the valley. The ranchers, always ready for more rain, often didn't get it, and there were hard times for them and the cows. So over the years the valley came to be known as "Sufferin' Springs Valley." As one old-timer said, "The valley is just as dusty and dried-up as the old springs are, and it'll take another 'forty days and forty nights' to grow anythin' here." But the old man was wrong, and now the valley is lush with lettuce, grain, cotton, cattle, and some new land developments that you wouldn't believe. But I sometimes wish the valley had remained like it was before.

Introduction

I AM SURE that many a person on their way through the dusty streets of Willcox in those days, even in these days, would ask why anyone in their right mind would live in such a place. Of course, one very attractive aspect of Willcox then was the large trees, which really did give the town the appearance of a lush mecca in the desert — until you were right in town. Then that image got tarnished somewhat, especially with the dusty streets, a few overgrown vacant lots, and so on. All in all, it just did not seem that this was a great place to live — but it was.

In order to set the stage for the following chapters, I must try to make you feel that you are really there in those days, to feel the atmosphere, the attitudes, and the tempo of this small town in the Southwest. And, of course, I certainly know that Willcox was the true focal point of the valley.

Willcox was really two towns. It was a raw-boned, tough, wild and woolly, "old-time West" town with carousing cowboys, cattlemen, railroaders, and construction workers (as the highway began to be built); and then it was also a very civilized town, with churches, civic clubs, and women's clubs like those found in every small city. The parents supported the schools and their children in everything, and the churches were full on Sunday and on prayer-meetin' night. There was genuine concern for one another. The pool halls and the gambling rooms in the back of the saloons on Saturday night did a great business. And speaking of business, everyone knew everyone else's business, or thought they did, or else they dreamed it up. The whole town closed down for a local citizen's funeral, and everything also closed down when the high school teams played in most sports.

A real treat every weekend was to attend the dances that were held in town or all over the valley in the small rural schoolhouses as money-making ventures for the local PTA. There were always some really good knockdown bloody brawls at these, either over somebody's girl or just to blow off some steam from the past workweek.

It was, to say the least, an exciting little town to grow up in. I can never forget the long, long trains that came through town at tremendous speeds, night and day. It took me a long time to get used to the quiet at night when I went off to college in Tucson. One of the unforgettable sights that is sadly no longer with us was the huge herds of cattle that were brought every spring and every fall in long trail drives to the shipping pens just outside of town. The railroad would bring in hundreds and hundreds of cattle cars to ship the cattle, and night after night for weeks, we went to bed to the bawling of hundreds of cattle out there in those pens. This part of western lore is no longer with us, but if you've ever experienced it, you'll never forget it.

As in every small town, you had to gain acceptance, but once you were a part of the scene, you were like a member of a very large family. It was all right to fight among yourselves, but just let a stranger get embroiled with one of the locals, and he had to fight the whole town.

Then there was the weather — and how can you describe that! Cold in the winter, even to the point of snowing now and again. The mountains, after the clouds lifted, would be completely white — and magnificent. There were the dust storms in the spring and summer, especially from the south. It seemed that the whole Dry Lake (a large alkali flat to the south of town) would come into town, ruining the wash on the line, sifting into the smallest crack or crevice. My mother never did get used to the dust; it was endless. The sunsets over the Winchester mountains, sometimes framed or enhanced by clouds turned gold, red, silver, or purple, truly were God's handiwork. The rains would come in the late summer, and the whole landscape turned green with the growing grass. The hillsides were one riot of color, completely covered with orange poppies, blue and purple lupine, and pink desert hollyhock. Out along the farm roads were miles and miles of huge sunflowers. If you went into the mountains around the valley you were surrounded on every side with the many varieties and colors of the wildflowers. In large areas of the valley, the grass would grow so high that a cow grazing could barely be seen above the tops of the grass. In fact, I can remember that the ranchers even baled that tall grass. Then would come the fall, when the grass dried up and turned brown and we settled down to the bleakness of winter and the dust, again.

One particular phenomenon that occurred every year during the rainy season was a nice little flood. Willcox sits on a sloping terrain, and we always had some real downpours. The water would gather in the small washes and gullies to the north of the town, gather momentum and volume, and come roaring down into town. Because of the gentle southern slope of the town, the water drained rapidly and would not get too high as it coursed its way through the main streets of town. Sometimes there would be some damage to stores, homes and other establishments, but not that much. Everyone knew this flood would happen, as it had since the town was begun, so the business people kept sand bags and other supplies in their stores, ready at a moment's notice to protect their property.

To us kids, though, this was fun! We would get an old washtub or some similar

Dos Cabezas Mountains (COURTESY "ARIZONA RANGE NEWS," WILLCOX)

type of makeshift boat, an old broom for rudder and oar, and away we went, floating along with the current down Railroad Avenue through town. The water would only be a foot or two deep, so we were never in any kind of trouble. Boy, how we looked forward to the rains.

But, as in all good things, the town fathers got tired of this and prevailed on either the county or the state (I don't remember which) to come in and build large dikes above the northern edge of town to divert the water. And so our yearly boat trips came to an end.

There were many fun times. Often at noon, and usually after school, if I wasn't working, I would join many of the other kids my age at the White Spot for a bowl of chili, a hamburger or a hot dog — none of them like any you would ever find today anywhere. The White Spot was a cafe in a very small building in the middle of the block on the main street. It was presided over quite ably by a diminutive but very competent Mrs. Cornet.

A few doors away was the town's theater, and, man, we saw all the good Westerns starring Ken Maynard, Tim McCoy, Hopalong Cassidy — you name it. We always had Saturday matinees with Flash Gordon and the like. Sunday afternoon was a great time to go to the movies — all the kids were there. And right next to the movie theater was the Sweet Shop, a place for the in-crowd to meet after the movie or a ball game, for a favorite milk shake, a Coke or any other kind of concoction we could get Mr. Rix to dish up.

There were also the mountains and the valley around the town, for picnics, hiking, horseback trips, and just plain exploring. No one had much money, so everyone had a part-time job somewhere. I carried the morning paper, played in dance bands, and worked in two different grocery stores — with the stipulation, of course, that I got off for football, basketball, or baseball practice and games. Since everything closed up when we high schoolers played a home game, I really wasn't missing work.

Of course, there was always the touch of the Old West with the cowboys and the cattlemen coming to town — and don't forget a few farmers. We did have some dry-land farms in the area then, and farmers came to town to shop and to trade produce and crops for food, clothing, and other necessities and a few luxuries. Saturday was an exciting day, and the stores, saloons, and pool halls did a tremendous business.

There was a true feeling of history in the town and in the valley. Many of the old-timers in town and the old-time ranchers had been there to fight the Apache or to know the Earps, Curly Bill, or some other outlaw or gunman. And there were old ghost towns all around the valley. In those days there was a lot left in them. They had not been torn down and ransacked as they are now. I can well remember walking down many an old boardwalk past the local barber shop, saloon, general store, churches, houses, and so on, in the likes of Pearce, Courtland, Gleason, Mascot, Paradise, and others. The old forts were there too. Fort Grant to the north (then the School for Boys for the state), with many original buildings remaining, Fort Bowie in Apache Pass to the east, Dragoon Springs in the Dragoon Mountains to the south, and Camp Rucker in the Chiricahuas. All you had to do was just listen to tales of the oldsters and you were right back there with them, always realizing that those days were not that far removed.

What kind of a town was Willcox? Well, it was just about anything and everything to a boy growing up in those days.

Introduction

Just the other day there was an article on Willcox in the daily paper in Phoenix, talking about life in a small town. Well, as far as I am concerned, the writer of that piece missed the whole point completely. Sure, Willcox is changed, as is every other town in this United States, but this article was way off base. All the article talked about were the problems of drugs and alcohol among the young people and their apparent boredom. I could go on quite a discourse on that, but I won't. Anyway, suffice it to say that the writer did not talk to any of the older people nor did he or she even attempt to find the good things still present in our small town. Of course, I am perhaps somewhat prejudiced.

The young people of my time found our days filled with activities. Most we did on our own, such as playing tennis and golf, horseback riding, having picnics, camping, or playing a pick-up game of touch football on the high school lawn. We had a ball and we never did think of ourselves as small-town "hicks" because, after all, we went to the big city of Tucson to shop occasionally. And, through activities in school, many of us traveled extensively — at least relative to that day. I do not ever remember, when any of my group got ready to go to college or to the service, that we were in the least overawed or overwhelmed. It just seemed that we were ready for the next chapter, and our attitude was, "Let's get on with it." I guess that came from the upbringing of a knowledgeable, understanding, and loving group of parents. And by no means do I leave out the wonderful people of that little town who backed and supported us in everything we did. They saw in our generation a great storehouse for future leadership, young people of which the parents and the town could be proud. I say, today, that those people did a great job and that they can be proud of their handiwork, because the boys and girls of Willcox in my day have gone on to reach heights that no one could have imagined in their wildest dreams.

Well, I won't argue with that recent article, which was written in 1976, but I can tell you that that article could never have even been conceived of in the thirties or forties; not about Willcox, Arizona, the "Cattle Capital of the World" and the hub of Sulphur Springs Valley!

We Arrive

I N 1934 the Depression was in full swing, and my family and I were living on a small farm just outside Glendale, Arizona, then a small town some nine miles from Phoenix. After pioneering agriculture education in the state, my dad had formed a consultant and management company in Phoenix with several of his old college friends. We were doing quite well, and Dad was even beginning to invest in land in the area. But one evening he came home and collapsed on the front doorstep, and we found out that he had pernicious anemia, a fatal disease in those days. Dad fought it with all his might and tried to carry out his regular work schedule, but this did not help his condition. Finally, the doctors stated flatly that we would have to get out of the heat and the low altitude of Phoenix. So Dad took the only job he could find in those days, county agent of Cochise County, and we were to live in Willcox in Sulphur Springs Valley.

This news was total disaster to all of us. Mother loved her home and the people around her. The unknown was staring at her because neither she, nor any one of us, had ever heard of Willcox. I was crushed; I loved the little farm, and I was involved in the 4-H club and had started quite a dairy herd with some purebred Jerseys. And I would miss my friends. My brother Dick was just a baby and my sister Carol was only about five when we had to go.

We said goodbye to the lush green Salt River Valley and headed east — to what? Everything was all right, considering, until we left Tucson. Then we were soon on a dirt road — a main highway, if you will — and it was getting drier and dustier by the mile. And it was cold. It was November, and the desert and hills were bleak and cold. The dust seeped into the car, and it was terrible!

We passed through the little town of Benson and headed up into some mountains, the Dragoons, as Dad told us. There we were in some of the most fascinating rock formations we had ever seen. We dropped down into the village of Dragoon, following the main line of the Southern Pacific Railroad, and began to head for the opening in the hills. Out ahead we could see a flat valley and a large range of mountains with two peaks at the top, the *Dos Cabezas* (Two Heads). We twisted and turned and went through a low underpass. Coming out on top of the grade, we looked across the most barren piece of land I had ever seen. Just beyond this was a group of trees and just a hint of greenery and civilization, and Dad exclaimed, "There it is, that's Willcox!" Mother never said a word, and neither did we kids. It looked like the end of the world. We passed through another little dry, dusty village known as Cochise and soon started out over an overpass. When we got on top, Dad stopped the car. Directly below us was a completely barren, flat alkali valley that stretched away for miles but soon appeared to be a beautiful lake. We all yelled at the sight of the water, but Dad soon put a damper on any enthusiasm. This was the Willcox Dry Lake, said by some to be the most perfect mirage ever seen in this hemisphere. How authentic it looked was proven by later events.

We piled back into the car and headed for what now could be seen as a town. Out across the barren, flat alkali into the dusk of evening we approached the trees. Soon we were near some homes that were dotted here and there with no apparent reason. The roads in the city went in every direction. It seemed that if you needed a road somewhere, it just got built in that direction. Of course, all the streets were dirt, and the only greenery of any consequence was the large cottonwoods and elms all over town. We headed down a street with an occasional house that followed alongside the tracks and finally led into a small business district, which covered several city blocks. The main business buildings were built next to the railroad tracks but separated from them by a small park. Dad said that we were going to the drugstore to get some medicine and that he would buy us a treat before we went on to a hotel. (You see, Dad had been here before us and made arrangements for our arrival.)

We went into a very old, quaint drugstore and found a booth. The young lady who waited on us was just about my age, and we eyed each other warily. Her dad owned the store, and she worked there after school. We were introduced all around, and then a treat of all treats was put before us kids — a milk shake. It tasted good after the dusty trip. Dad told us later that the drugstore had been right there since the late 1800s, and I certainly believed that!

We then headed outside. We kids were in for something, the likes of which we had not seen, except from a distance — it was snowing! We couldn't believe it — not in Arizona. We gathered our things and ran into the hotel and up the stairs to a small lobby. There were two women there who greeted us. One turned out to be the owner and the other, a schoolteacher. Again, the introductions, and then we found our rooms. We kids were dead to the world. After that pioneering journey, who cared about food?

The next day the scene was beautiful. All the bleakness and barrenness was covered by snow. Dad had to go to work. He had to have a shot for his anemia every day, besides taking all kinds of pills. I could see how worried, tense, and tired he was.

2

Cook Hotel, where we spent our first nights in Willcox
(COURTESY "ARIZONA RANGE NEWS," WILLCOX)

We stayed at this small hotel for several days. During that time, Dad took us down the other main drag about a block, and next to a small cafe and service station was an old stuccoed adobe house, with a yard but no grass. This, he announced, was to be home. And that wasn't all: the old man who owned the house went with it. It was this house or nothing. Mother had tears in her eyes.

Two days later, our furniture arrived and we moved in. The old man stayed in a small apartment that adjoined our kitchen, but many times he ate with us. He was a nice old gentleman, but not the tidiest, and Mother had to clean up after him as much as she did after us kids. It was a burden on her.

We Arrive

Finally came the day for me to go to school. The old grade school was just two blocks from my home and down the main drag. The architect for the school system in Willcox had quite an imagination. The grade school consisted of one main building with one large dome in the center of it. The high school, in the center of town, was constructed the same way, except that it had two domes. I suppose that to show the progress you made, you went from one to two domes.

The kids in the seventh grade with me were not different from anywhere else, but I was considered a definite outsider and had to prove myself. It had never entered my mind that the proof was to consist of engaging in battle with all of the boys in the class. One each day met me with all of the other boys in the class, and I was challenged. I think I might add that, to my credit, I was able to prove myself with all of them. It did take me several times with one of the boys who lived across the street from me. After all this, I was accepted as one of them, but only when it came to school. Of course, my mother was beside herself with all of the bloody noses, lips, and so on, and the torn clothes, but this was the only way to settle down to school.

It was a strange town: friendly, yet wary, and it seemed that we were a long way from being one of the townspeople. I think we were considered "city folk," and the populace watched and waited to see how we would act or react.

I could go into a long discourse about all of the events that happened in the first years in Willcox, but this would not serve my purpose. Needless to say, there were trials and tribulations with the old house, the old man, Dad's illness, and the continuing effort of the family to really become Willcox-ites.

Finally, an event took place in our lives that, tragic though it was, changed everything considerably.

After we had lived in the old house for over a year, Dad found a nice little three-bedroom frame house, clear up on the other side of town. This wasn't bad for me because it was within easy walking-distance to the high school. Of course, Carol had to be taken to school. Dick was still too young.

We were very happy in this little house, and we had neighbors, for a change. I had a job delivering the *Arizona Daily Star* early in the mornings, and I began to play in a high school dance band, even as a freshman. The kids at school were much friendlier. But as far as we were concerned, we still had not achieved that feeling of belonging. But then, one Saturday in the spring, Dad came home to tell us that he had bought us a home. We bundled into the car to ride down to see it. What a beautiful big house and yard, and right across the street from the grade school! We were so excited that we could hardly sleep that night. The next day, Sunday, we went to church, came home to the usual Sunday dinner, and then went our separate ways. I knew that several of the kids would be on

4

Willcox Grammar School (COURTESY "ARIZONA RANGE NEWS," WILLCOX)

the tennis courts over by the school, so I went there to join them, dressed very fashionably in a brand new white slack suit. That evening I was to play in the high school band for the baccalaureate service for the graduating seniors.

Suddenly the town's fire siren started. We all searched the horizon for telltale smoke but could see none. We could hear the fire truck heading our way. I yelled to the others, "Go ahead and play, it's probably a false alarm — there's been a bunch this past week." We turned back to tennis. Suddenly someone yelled, "Bliss, it's over by your house!" I took off running.

When I was some four blocks away I could see the black smoke billowing up where our house was. Then I saw my folks in our car, careening up the street ahead of me. I ran as I have never run before — and it was our house. When I got there, the house was completely aflame. Several pieces of furniture were out in front where the fireman had been able to get them, but just a few pieces piti-fully remained of all our worldly belongings. My mother was crying as if her

5

heart would break, and even Dad had tears in his eyes as we watched everything burn.

Before the fire was even close to being put out, people surrounded us, comforting us. Offers of help came from all sides. When we realized that nothing more could be done there, we took the offer of rooms from several friends and went to their house. The next day we moved into the Willcox Hotel as free guests of the two gentlemen who owned it. There were offers of food, clothing, financial help, and genuine sympathy. For indeed, our world had crumbled about us.

In the next few days and weeks, when we had time to realistically appraise our situation and set about doing something about it, we all suddenly knew that, in the tragedy of the moment, we had been accepted as one of the "family" that was Willcox. We had, indeed, arrived.

My First Job

ALL BOYS, at one time or another, become paperboys, and so did I. Shortly after we had moved to the house that eventually burned down, I got the money "bug" and started looking for a job. At this time I was in the eighth grade and all of thirteen years old, but I felt pretty big because the eighth grade classes were held in the high school building.

I don't recall who started the ball rolling, but one afternoon after school I found a Mr. McCoy on my doorstep. He was the man in charge of all the paper-boys outside of Tucson for the *Arizona Daily Star,* the morning paper. He had heard that I was looking for something, and the local route was available immediately. I was ready! But he insisted that I talk to my parents and advise them of all the ins and outs. He was staying at one of the local hotels (Willcox had two hotels, which was something) and would await my decision the next day. So Mother and Dad and I discussed it. Dad was not too keen about me getting up at four-thirty, rain or shine, to deliver the papers. I am sure that he could envision himself along with me on many a rainy or snowy day. But it was decided that I could take the job. I was to start the following Sunday and go around with the present paperboy to learn the route.

I can remember that the first Sunday was exciting and that I was awake long before the alarm went off. It was spring — beautiful and balmy. I have to admit that there would be other days when I would not feel that the early morning was that beautiful.

The papers came by train. In those days, four passenger trains went through Willcox going east and four going west. Only two from each direction stopped, however, unless there were passengers getting on or off. We were on the main line of the Southern Pacific. The eastbound "Argonaut" came through about 4:10 a.m., and the baggage clerk would simply open the door and throw out the large bundles of papers as the train whistled through. And it whistled through at about seventy or eighty miles per hour! We stood back and gave him plenty of room so we wouldn't be hit — that is, if we were there soon enough to meet the train.

When my career started, it was fun, at first. Then fall came, and it was very, very dark in the early morning. I began to be a worried character on those dark mornings. Up until fall my route did not take me too far out in the boondocks, but then my route changed, and I had to go way out to several very isolated houses. One of these was the town's haunted house. I guess every town has one. There was a lady living in the house who was said to be crazy, and many weird stories had been told about her. The house was a large two-story with two wings and a staircase in the middle of the main room, which I could see at early light through the windows. Her house was off by itself on the east side of the railroad tracks, a good two or three blocks from any other house.

All spring and summer it was light when I went to the house, and I threw the paper and hightailed it as fast as I could. When I collected, the money was always left in the mailbox in the front of the house. But here I was in fall having to deliver the paper in the dark. I soon hit upon an idea, to deliver that paper the very last — even though it meant having to go back clear across town to do it. But I wasn't about to go near that house in the dark.

Finally, however, I had to come to grips with that house and its lone occupant. When the money wasn't in the mailbox one month, I just let it go. But then the next month came and went, and still no money. Mr. McCoy, who came to Willcox once in a while to help me, noticed the long-overdue bill. He chided me and coaxed me into going to the house for the money. I couldn't get my Dad's help — he said that it was my job and that nothing would happen anyway. It took me several weeks to get up my nerve.

One afternoon I mustered all the courage I could and went to the house. I walked up to the door, shaking to pieces, and timidly knocked, fully expecting something terrible to happen. Nothing happened. I knocked again, and, again, nothing happened, when suddenly in back of me a deep voice lashed out, "Little boy, what do you want?" I whirled around, and there beside me was the biggest, most unkempt woman I had ever seen. Her dark eyes flashed at me and she asked again, "What do you want?" I wanted to run, but my legs had turned to rubber and wouldn't function, so I just stood there, shaking, my teeth rattling. She glared at me, and I was finally able, in a very small, shaking voice, to tell her about the bill. With this, she broke into a great laugh, shaking all over with her laughter, and said, "Come in, I've been waiting for you."

I didn't want to go in there for love nor money. I told her I would wait outside, but she would have none of it. She led the way into a large front room with the great staircase, and then off to the side to the kitchen. This was also a huge room, and I noticed that all the furniture, fixtures, and appliances were all very old. I was scared to death. She ordered me to sit at the table and said, "Little boy, you're scared of me." I answered, "No," but my heart wasn't in it and she knew it, and she roared again with laughter. I wanted to be anywhere else but there.

She disappeared into another part of the kitchen, I suppose a pantry, and returned with some change. She counted it out for me, but as I reached for it, she pulled it back and said that I would not get the money until I promised to deliver her paper earlier. This, it seems, had been the reason she had not paid. I promised as I had never promised before. When I reached for the money again, she pulled it back again and said, "Wait." She disappeared once more but returned with a big slice of cold watermelon. She ordered me to eat it, and I did. While I ate, she asked me all about my family and everything else she could think of, and I realized that the "crazy lady" was just a lonely and very pathetic person — she just wanted to visit.

I left that house with a completely different outlook on life. Never again was I going to be scared over just someone else's tall tales. I vowed I would not pass on untrue stories about someone else. Yes, maybe that lady was a little strange, but so would anyone else be that lived as she did and had to endure the feelings of the townspeople toward her.

My career as a paperboy sailed on, and my route grew and grew. Some people said I was a natural born salesman. I sold paper subscriptions every chance I got, and the paper sponsored a number of contests, and I won my share. But I did have one other adventure that left a lasting impression on me.

As I said previously, Willcox was still a pretty raw-boned town in those days, and even if it was the Depression, a lot of money changed hands at the card tables in the saloons and on the tables of the pool halls in town. Willcox was a rural town and a cow town. The cowboys and farmers came into town on Saturdays to do hard drinking and gambling. Oh, yes, it was all very illegal, but no one paid much attention to that fact. But as you might suspect, there were a lot of hard feelings at times.

We kids were cautioned about ever entering a pool hall or saloon, but I can remember sneaking into one on Front Street one Saturday afternoon. I saw several thousand in cash, a horse, and a Buick sedan change hands during one game of "nine-ball."

Well, one of those cold dark mornings, just as winter was turning into spring, I was on my route as usual. By this time, I was a sophomore in high school and quite a business tycoon, because I had another boy working for me. On this day, he was waiting for me in the middle of town where there was a service station that opened early and had a cafe next to it. We were meeting there to have a cup of hot chocolate.

I was on my bicycle, about a block away, paying no attention to anything directly in front of me. I was looking up toward the station to see if Ed was there. About that time I hit something on the sidewalk, and I went rear-end-over-appetite. I got up and felt myself all over to see about broken bones. When I started to pick up the bike, I looked down at the body of a man stretched across the sidewalk. His face, or what was left of it, was down in the gutter, and there was blood everywhere. I couldn't move — I was petrified. Finally, I started running and yelling at the same time. Ed and the man at the service station started toward me. When they realized what I was saying, we went back and checked the body again. The service station attendant went to call the deputy sheriff and the town constable. When they got there, I finally settled down. The deputy, Mr. Tucker, asked me all kinds of questions and told me that I would probably have to appear at an inquest hearing.

I'll never forget that hearing. Right across the street from where I had found the body was a combination furniture store and funeral parlor. The undertaker was Mr. Rottman, which I guess was an appropriate name. All the local officials were there, as well as a coroner's jury and the body covered by a sheet. It was all very solemn. I was questioned as to what time I found the man, his position in the street, and some other questions that I don't remember. I do remember that I was tickled to death to get out of there. I heard later that the result of this hearing stated that the man had died at the hands of someone unknown. I do not believe to this day that that murder has ever been solved. The officials knew that he had been gambling in a back room of a liquor store very late that night, but no other information was ever found. All of this made me quite a celebrity at school.

My so-called salesmanship must have been present all those years, because I always seemed to win the subscription contests each time I entered. The paper was always sponsoring some type of trip for the carriers if you signed up so many new customers. So every day after school I beat the bushes for new people to subscribe to the paper. The first time I entered, I won a trip to the Grand Canyon for three days in the summer. This was the start of quite a friendship between two other carriers from other parts of the state and myself. One of the boys was a big, tall, black-haired boy whose mother was a state legislator from Hayden. The other was a short, stocky, wavy-haired comedian, if I ever knew one, from Ajo. Warren Rosenbaum and Malcolm Jones, respectively. What a time we had! Mr. Paul McCoy, the circulation manager, and his wife became friends, counselors, finance managers, and anything else needed. The McCoys had quite an effect on my life. They were fine people, and I thought that Mrs. McCoy was probably the prettiest woman I had ever seen.

The next trip sponsored by the paper was to see the Rose Bowl and the Rose Parade in Pasadena, California. Again, the three of us won the trip. We traveled to San Diego first and went aboard several Navy ships and saw the San Diego Zoo and other places of interest there. Then we headed up the coast, stopping to see all the sights. We finally landed on New Year's Eve at the New Rossylyn Hotel, right in the heart of downtown Los Angeles. Well, this was quite a deal for a fourteen-year-old kid right out of Willcox, Arizona, population 890 happy souls and one *crank* — to be in Los Angeles in the first place, but to be there on New Year's Eve! The place was a madhouse, with people everywhere. The excitement was something! The University of Alabama was playing California, and the hotel was full of both schools' rooters, most of them feeling no pain by early evening. Our chaperon let us roam around the hotel to mingle with the others and go in and out of the various ballrooms. You see, the New Rossylyn Hotel consisted of two large buildings, one on each side of the street, with a tunnel underneath the street to connect them.

One gentleman, on finding out that I had a ticket to the game, offered me one hundred dollars for it. That was a lot of money to me, but I turned it down because I wasn't going to miss any of this, no matter what. I might never get this kind of chance again.

In order to get out to Pasadena in time for the parade, we were told to get up early on New Year's Day. We had breakfast and were on the Pacific Electric train at five-thirty in the morning, headed for the festivities. It took us eleven miles and until nine o'clock to get to our destination, the Union Station in downtown Pasadena. We had seats on the top of it to see the parade. And what a sight! I don't believe I have to describe this to anyone who has seen it on television. In those days there was no time limit, and the marchers were still going by at one o'clock when we had to walk over to the Rose Bowl for the game. The Bowl sits on the far side of a large grassy valley and does not look too prepossessing until you get to it and then, when you go through the tunnel and look down, down, down onto the field, then you are really impressed! I had never seen so many people at one time, in one place, in all of my life. The excitement was electric! I had my hopes riding on Alabama, but all of my cheering and the banners didn't help a bit, and the Californians won. But to top off all the excitement, Mickey Rooney and his group were sitting close by.

We stayed on one more day to see more of the sights. Then I went home and went before the entire high school student body and the local Rotary Club to tell of my wonderful adventure.

One more trip became the highlight of my paperboy career. It was quite a trip and took a lot of doing to win it. But win it I did! We went to California again, but this time we toured the movie studios and actually went on the sets while they were making pictures. As usual, Warren and Malcolm and I made the trip. We took many trips to the Pike, a large amusement park on the ocean in Long Beach, and other side trips, but we couldn't wait to get to Hollywood!

My First Job

The first day was a tour of **MGM**. We were shown around the lots where all the different types of sets were. We were also shown the very famous Marie Dressler dressing room, actually a house all by itself in the middle of the lot and kept as she had had it in her heyday. Just before noon we were on the set of *Stand Up and Fight*, starring Wallace Beery and Robert Taylor. We watched them film an airplane crashing in the mountains, using model planes and miniature mountains. If you remember these old movies, you may remember scenes like that, stirring music and all. Next we were escorted to the cafeteria where we sat down to lunch around a great large table with Franchot Tone, George Murphy, Robert Taylor, and Wallace Beery. We were dazzled! I don't remember eating a thing. . . . That afternoon we went on the set of *Honolulu*, starring George Burns, Gracie Allen, and Eleanor Powell, among others. They were in the midst of shooting a shipboard scene with the orchestra and the sound-effects and Miss Powell doing her dancing. After the scene was over, we had our pictures taken with her and a group of boys visiting from Boys State. We also had our pictures taken with Burns and Allen. Then that day was over.

But the next day was another thing. We started the day by going onto the set of *The Wizard of Oz* and saw the filming of the Cowardly Lion, the Tin Man, the Scarecrow, and Dorothy making their way to the Emerald City. Dorothy, of course, was played by Judy Garland. (I've seen many reruns of this on television and still get goose bumps, remembering.) After lunch we went to the Hal Roach Studios to have our pictures taken with Laurel and Hardy, Jean Parker, and Douglas Shearer (Norma Shearer's brother) on the set of *It's Spring Again*. We watched a scene involving Laurel, Hardy, and Stepin Fetchit. The climax to the day was to take a ride in the car used in the *Topper* movies when the driver was supposed to be invisible. Of course, the driver lay on his stomach and looked out through the grill. This ended our studio tour, and we headed for home. As before, I recounted my experiences to the school, the Rotary Club, and several other organizations that I cannot remember. In those days, entertainment was where you found it. But I'll say this, for a small-town kid I was running in pretty worldly circles — thanks to the *Arizona Daily Star*.

We Play for Experience

MUSIC WAS ALWAYS a part of my life. I inherited the love of music from my mother and dad. Dad had played the trumpet and the french horn all the way through college, and I can't remember a day that he didn't sing in the church choir. And Mother was something else — she had studied music all the way through school and was considered a concert pianist and violinist. She was always the church organist or pianist, depending on the financial status of the church we were attending at the time. So I grew up with all types of musical instruments and sheet music and voices raised in song. Mother always gave music lessons: in voice, violin, piano, and most anything else.

When I was in the third grade, Dad gave me his trumpet and started me out with lessons given at the school. The trumpet had quite a history: it had been played by a soloist in the John Phillip Sousa Band, and the soloist had had a heart attack and died while playing it. His wife, who knew my grandparents, gave the trumpet to my dad. Dad was very young then. He learned to play it, and he played it until the day he gave it to me. My very first day of tryouts on the trumpet almost ended my musical career, when the music teacher told me that I did not have the proper type of mouth to play the trumpet and would be better off playing a reed instrument such as a clarinet. Dad stated flatly that he wasn't going to listen to any "squeaking clarinet" and kept me at the trumpet. I've often wondered what that music teacher (still a very close friend) would have said years later if he had heard me play, because I did achieve a certain amount of ability on that old instrument.

By the time I arrived in Willcox, I had been playing for about four years. As an eighth grader I was recruited into the high school band. At that time, Willcox Union High School had an enrollment of one hundred ten kids, including the eighth grade, so everyone did everything, including playing in the band. At the same time, Mother was making sure that I kept a singing voice. She taught me some voice and encouraged me to sing in the school chorus, the youth choir, and anywhere else that a group got up to sing.

In the spring of my freshman year, a group of us got together for the purpose of forming a dance band and earning our first million. We knew that, with our talent, there could be no stopping us. The leader of our group was Clifford Keeth, a very mature senior and worldly man-about-town. He played the sax, led us in every way, and made all the business arrangements. The other sax man was Bill McAleb, always one of my best friends, whom I envied because of his ability to do just about anything. The girls thought Bill was something else. To complete the so-called "front-line" was the trumpet player — me. On the rhythm guitar was Bill Duncan, who played with us from time to time. Many times, because of the prices we charged, we would only allow five to play. On drums we had George Takagi, whose mother was Mexican and his dad, Japanese. He had more rhythm and ability on the drums than anyone who has ever played with us since. George was a real character. We began by having many, many practice sessions with and without sheet music. Now, when I say sheet music I am not talking about wonderful, long, and complicated arrangements by the likes of Benny Goodman or Charlie Barnett. We had piano sheet music, and I had to transpose and play by ear. With time, we set about making our own arrangements — again, by ear. We also had to have a gimmick, so we made some really nice music stands and painted them white. Then we painted on them a swing with a treble cleff on it and, in glowing letters, "Cliff and His Swinging Cleffs." We were ready!

Digressing a bit, I must relate that I continued to play in the high school band and sometimes in an orchestra. I played under several music teachers, and I achieved success as a soloist and in a brass quartet, trumpet trio, and other groups that were gotten together from year to year to participate in music festivals, concerts and so on.

Of course, the great challenge and the place where we were sure we would achieve success was our dance band. You have to understand that in those Depression days, everyone took their fun and recreation where and when they could get it. Certainly, one of the most popular pastimes of the day was dancing. Everyone — townspeople, ranchers, farmers, and of course, young people from all over the valley — almost lived from one weekend to the next waiting for the next dance. Every organization in every area of the valley knew that the way to make money for any cause, worthy or not so worthy, was to hold a dance. In the valley were small towns such as Bowie, San Simon, Elfrida, and Cochise. There also were many rural schools. When the PTAs, the American Legion, the Elks, churches of various denominations, women's clubs, and men's organizations all got into the act, almost every Friday and Saturday night you could find as many dances to go to as there were villages, hamlets, and rural schoolhouses. The whole family went. Always there was food — good and plentiful. It was really fun!

14

We Play for Experience

Into this great atmosphere of opportunity stepped Cliff and His Swinging Cleffs. We were greatly in demand, probably because there was such a lack of dance bands. People in the valley would dance to just about anything, including a full-sized group as we were, or just a fiddle, guitar, and maybe even a harmonica player, the guy keeping time with his feet.

I have to brag somewhat and say that we did a pretty good job, and we played just about every weekend. But I would stretch the truth if I said that we got wealthy — far from it! That's the reason we had the slogan on our stands, "We Play for Experience." And that was about right. But I must say that my paper route and playing in the band, and later, other jobs, kept me in clothes and spending money. And it was fun. We met a lot of fine people and, as is the want of high school boys, we checked out all the local girls pretty well. We couldn't dance with them or anything, but we sure got in a lot of looking and quite a little flirting as they danced by.

The very first job we got was when I was a freshman in school, at a dance held in Dos Cabezas. Some fifteen miles up in the Dos Cabezas Mountains was the little village of the same name. It had been quite a mining town in the early part of the century but was now sparsely populated with a few people who hung on in one way or another and a few miners still working some of the small gold mines in the area. The town consisted of many vacant houses, two general stores, a post office, a school, and a combination saloon and pool hall. A civic organization held this dance that we played at, and they moved all the pool tables out of the pool hall and proceeded. Well, it was Saturday night, and the miners and cowboys had all been paid. We were in for a *glorious* time. As the evening wore on, the crowd got well soused. The fights began and the bottles flew, and some high school dance band boys were getting darned scared! The dance was to be over at one o'clock, but everybody contributed to a passed hat and we were forced to play on. The crowd got more and more unruly and the hat was passed many times. We just knew we weren't going to come out of this alive. We tried to reason with the dancers, but that just made things worse. Finally, about half past four in the morning, one of the drunker participants staggered out on the dance floor and threw a whole pocketful of silver dollars (his week's pay) out on the dance floor. When the crowd dove for the money, we went out the back way, carrying our instruments, music, and other paraphernalia as we could. Our first dance was over. We had been very scared, but the money took care of that quickly, and we were ready to play again.

Well, I haven't the time nor space to tell you about all of the dances and the fabulous places we played, but we had fun, made some money, and I guess we did our part in providing some entertainment to the local populace. I do have to mention, however, some of the more memorable occasions, such as one of our experiences at Pearce. Pearce was an old gold mining town that lay some twenty-five miles from Willcox, near the Three Sisters Hills and in the foothills of the Dragoon Mountains. There was a general store, some occupied houses, and the schools. They were really "uptown," since they had a high school as well as a grade school. The center of everything was the old, old gathering place, Huddy Hall, built in the heyday of the town. No doubt it was named after some local celebrity of the day. The old hall was literally held up by two-by-fours propped up against the building all the way around. In the back were two outhouses, one for the men and one for the ladies. Inside was the large hall with a stage at the far end that had an old screen, covered with all types of advertising, that rolled up and down on a round pole.

As always, the dance participants were the locals, the ranchers nearby, and just about anyone from that part of the state who might want to get some "rootin' and tootin'." And again, as always, the local PTA put out a feed that wouldn't quit. They charged for it, of course, but that was just part of the whole thing, and they made their money this way. I remember that the specialty at Huddy Hall was Mexican food, and it was something else! Those people liked their music pretty much on the fast side. I mean, when they danced, they wanted to "get up and go." Man, that old hall would begin to rock. The floor would go up and down, and the walls would go in and out, and we often wondered whether or not there would be a building left when that piece was over.

We were really playing, and the dancing was getting wilder and wilder by the minute, when our fine sax man, Cliff, advised us of his need to visit the outhouse. He left by the back way, going up over the stage and out the old stage door. The rest of us carried on in fine style; we kept on and on and on and on, and still no Cliff. We finally called a hasty intermission and went looking for him. We got out back and yelled and hollered and ... nothing. Then one of the band yelled for quiet. "I think I hear something, be still a minute." We stopped, listened, and, sure enough, we could hear a voice off in the distance. In a most anguished tone, the voice of Cliff came to us, "Help, get me out!"

Well, you guessed it: he had fallen in. In getting him out, we had our friendship for a fellow human being in distress put to the ultimate test. We gritted our teeth and helped him get somewhat straightened out. Cliff rode on the outside of the car on the way home. What a way to end up a dance.

At these dances you could always count on at least one good fist fight. Usually these involved rivalry over a girl's favors. During the dances the participants were always seen to come and go, inside to outside and vice versa. Well, they weren't going out for a breath of fresh air. They were out there to do a little imbibing — a swallow or two of the "old dog." Then, about halfway through the dance, things would begin to warm up considerably. When two or more men decided to fight, to gain the favor of one of the belles-in-residence or just to wear off a little energy, the dance was discontinued while everyone took to the outside to watch the battlers. These fights were about as pugilistic as the participants were drunk. The drunker they were, the less damage done — if a blow was even struck. If you really had a good dance, why, there were several of these donnybrooks.

I guess the ultimate came one night when we were playing at the schoolhouse in Bonita, a junction in the road from Willcox to Fort Grant or turning west to Klondyke or east to Stockton Pass and Safford. We always enjoyed the dances in Bonita because a lot of the "dudes" from the 76 Ranch, up the way, would come. Those city girls were pretty good to look at, and the old cowboys really vied for their attentions. That night the local PTA was having a big feed and the place was crowded, and two of the cowpokes decided they liked the same girl. The girl liked all the attention and did nothing to prevent the inevitable, so we all adjourned outside for the big show. It was a mismatch from the very start. One man was really big, and he proceeded to render the other participant senseless in a matter of minutes. So we left the loser lying on the ground and returned to more pleasant pursuits. The dance came to an end. We packed our instruments, got our money and divided it, piled into the car, and headed for home. When leaving Bonita, one heads south for a short distance, then west on a ridge. As we got on the ridge road, we looked back and saw the school enveloped in flames. We turned the car around and headed back as fast as we could go. A bucket brigade had been formed, but it was no use — the school burned to the ground. Later we found that the disgruntled loser of the fight had awakened and decided to get some sort of satisfaction out of the evening by setting the schoolhouse on fire.

My dear and good parents — if they had known what went on at some of these weekly events, I am sure that my dance band career would have ended, and quickly. But as it was, they were not aware of all these things, and we went right on playing all through my high school days. I do say, though, to the credit of all of us in the band, that we did not drink nor get involved in some of the frivolity around us. After all, we were pros and were expected to act like it. Anyhow, it was fun, and it started me in a dance band career that didn't end until some twenty-five years later.

The Family

I CERTAINLY COULD NOT continue this story without telling about my family, and my mother and dad, in particular. These were two of the most wonderful people who ever lived, and they were the guiding light in my life. To really understand the times then, you have to know about the family life in a town like Willcox, and my parents were the essence of that life.

I want to include this part of the book especially for those of the younger generations and for those who feel that marriage and family life are not important to our society now. I have the perfect example in my parents and my family. Now, this isn't to say that we were the "perfect family" of our time, but I do want to show the beautiful love, affection, and understanding togetherness of our family led on by Mother and Dad.

My mother was a very pretty lady who tended to be a little on the plump side as she grew older. She was about five feet three inches tall with beautiful black hair streaked with gray. She had sharp features and very discerning hazel eyes. She could do anything. She was a great cook; I can almost taste some of her baking — there were always cookies, cake, pie, or something else in the oven. She could be the perfect hostess at any kind of gathering, yet she was equally at home on a camping trip, although I know that that type of activity was tolerated and not looked forward to by Mother. She was definitely not an outdoors girl in that respect. She loved the mountains, the valley, and the scenery but would rather do her eating and sleeping in a nice hotel or motel. But she was a good sport and put up with family outings that involved camping. But picnics were a different matter. She was ready for one at the drop of a hat, but then she was also ready to be back in her home come nightfall.

Elma Eileen Roewe Bliss was her name, and she did not learn to speak English until she went to grade school. Her dad was full German (my grandfather), and he spoke with an accent. My grandmother, a very pretty, gray-haired, plump little lady, was French and German. The Roewe name was definitely German and pronounced "ravey," or like "gravy." I strongly suspect, however, that a lot of Mother's personality was tempered from the stronger German attitudes, stubbornness, and so on, by the French blood in her. She was very, very affectionate with all of us, and she certainly was not the stubborn kind.

18

Mother loved music, which was a great part of her life. I cannot remember the day that the strains of music did not flow all through the house, with Mother at the piano and the violin. Mainly the piano got most of her attention, and she would play by the hour. She had graduated from the Music Conservatory in Kansas and then continued to learn and study further on her own. She was always the church pianist and organist in every town we lived. She gave all kinds of music lessons. I can remember coming home in the afternoon after school, and there would be some aspiring musician holding forth on the piano or violin, or even having a voice lesson. These voice lessons were really something, because my mother, with all of her musical talent, could not sing a note. She absolutely had no voice at all, but there she'd be, giving voice lessons. And she turned out some really fine musicians. One boy went on to become the student director of the West Point choir. A good friend of mine went on to appear on Broadway in a number of musicals, and to this day, he is still earning his way as a singer and television performer. Another friend, although not a bona fide student of Mother's, went on to become a well-known cowboy actor-singer. Rex Allen came to our house quite often for Mother to help him with his singing. She loved her music, and she was, to say the least, somewhat vain about it. By that I mean that she prized her role as the "leading musician of the town," playing at various functions at the drop of a hat. She was also, of course, the pianist-organist of the First Methodist Church. My mother took all this quite seriously. If another lady appeared in town who fashioned herself in this same role, Mother got very upset and concerned that her role was going to be challenged. But I do not ever remember that she lost her "queenly" position.

She loved us all, and she and my dad were like a couple of newlyweds all of their life together. They could visit by the hour, and they went for long walks together in the evenings. I well remember going to bed, and to sleep, with the low conversations of my mother and dad in the living room. It seemed that they could never talk themselves out; they always found each other interesting and exciting. They never were bored or tired with each other.

Now, my mother was not a disciplinarian; just the opposite. She could always see our side of the situation — us kids, that is — no matter what mischief we got into. She could get angry, but as I think back, I just cannot remember her angry at any of us, at any time. It was always someone outside the family. If they had done or said anything against any of us, then she was quick to anger, no matter what the circumstances. Perhaps this was a weakness, but it was very good and very pleasant as far as we kids were concerned. We always knew we had an ally in Mother. But let me be quick to add that we kids never ever got into any serious trouble, nor did we ever cause any serious discipline problems for our parents. I can probably attribute this fact to Dad, who was very different on the issue of discipline.

Mother passed on to me, they say, her outgoing nature and her talkativeness. She was always the leader in the group, always the hostess, and she loved people. She wanted people around her. She entertained church groups, or some of the neighbor ladies, or just any group that wanted to come. When we moved into the big house that really was "home" to us, she was delighted because it had a lot of room. The living and dining rooms were huge, made to order for her. Now she could entertain, and entertain she did. And she was good at it. I can well remember very large groups coming to our home, but it made no difference to Mother if the group was large or small. In fact, the larger the better. She always held the big tea and reception for the annual Cattlemen's Association Convention, to which all the wives came. She was a member of the "Cowbelles," the ladies auxiliary of that organization. In fact, the idea of the Cowbelles organization started in our front room at one of these gatherings. We had the governor and other dignitaries at our home on numerous occasions. Mother was equally at home with everyone. That may sound as if we were up there among the socially elite, when you have to remember that this was in fact a very young state where people knew others from all walks of life and from all over the state. My folks enjoyed everyone, and everyone was welcome at our home.

But everything was certainly not peaches and cream like it may sound. We had all the necessities of life, but money was not plentiful, and my mother worried about the finances and, of course, about Dad. His pernicious anemia continued unabated, and he kept the doctors and the druggist in business. But he lived a good life, as far as anyone could tell; most people, even close friends and associates, just did not know that he was sick. We kids were not aware of the problem's seriousness until we were fully grown. Life went on around us, and Dad always seemed in good health and in good spirits. So we were just not that concerned. It was an amazing thing, as I look back, that he did live such a good life. But Mother worried, and then, too, the parcels of land and other property we had acquired down in the Salt River Valley had to be sold, one by one and piece by piece, until there was nothing left.

It happened very rarely, but sometimes I would see tears in Mother's eyes. She would hastily brush them out and smile when caught like this and make small talk, but at those times I realized just how serious this part of our life was. Once in a while I would hear Mother and Dad talking about the sad state of our finances. Since Dad was taking all that medicine every day, the cost was a real burden. And our fire had not helped the situation, of course.

My mother was a rare person indeed. She was beautiful, inside and out. She

20

In front, Dick and Carol. In back, Mother, me, and Dad

was generous to a fault. She was one of the kindest people I ever knew. And how she loved her family and her home, I hesitate to try to describe. In the last few months of her life, she did not complain once. She had cancer two times, and the pain was unbearable for her, but she made not one whimper or complaint. The nurses and doctors fell in love with her — they didn't need to cheer her, she cheered *them*. She lived the last six years of her life with a colostomy, which I am sure was a real burden, but still she made no complaints.

I cannot think of my mother without remembering her in her garden. I can still see her out there in her flowers, puttering around, handling each plant with loving care. Her gardens and flowers were her pride and joy, and she was very generous with her flowers. Many people enjoyed bouquets of flowers on their tables or mantels, for no special reason except that Mother just gave them. She felt that people should enjoy the beauty of plants and flowers.

Here I am, now, in the later years of life, and it is still hard to realize that this delightful, sweet lady has been gone all these years. My mother died at the age of 51. My oldest child, Abby, who was only three months old at the time, was the only grandchild she ever saw or knew. I can imagine the wonderful love and the wonderful times she would have had with all the fifteen grandchildren that eventually made up our family. I know that there is a very special place in heaven for her and that she is there now. I hope she has a garden to putter in.

Dad, of course, had a very different personality. But like my mother, he was very affectionate with the family. Oh, I don't mean that he went around hugging us boys, but he could just flash that grin at us and we knew where we stood with him. Dad was the disciplinarian, and he certainly kept us in line. I can only remember once that he ever paddled me, however, or used any physical force, and that was because I had talked back to him in a very sarcastic way. I don't know of anything that could get him more angry than to have any of us "back-talk" him. When he got angry, we could see his face begin to get red and knew the storm was gathering. Then it was time to take a different "tack" or suffer the consequences. He was a quiet man, really, a very dignified man who commanded respect. We kids just naturally learned early in life that he was a father to be trusted and a father to listen to, and so we simply did not do things that might disappoint or antagonize him. I rather feel that the best word to use here is "disappoint." We felt that to disappoint Dad was some type of betrayal. So if there was one consideration in our lives that made us behave and to try to do the right thing, it was not to disappoint our dad. I know this sounds like we were a bunch of goodie-goodies but that was not the case, ever. We had a good time and did our share of mischief-making, but never anything extreme or drastic that might cause real concern to either Dad or Mother.

Only now, in these later years of my life, can I understand or have any type of comprehension about the seriousness of my dad's illness. And it is only now that I fully realize that my dad was only an arm's-length away from death just about every day of his life. What if I had that kind of burden? Could I have lived the kind of life he did? I don't think so. In fact, I just don't know anyone who could. When my dad passed away, many, many close friends came up to me later and wanted to know what type of cancer he had had. They never knew the burden he carried — very few knew. Some of the doctors knew and, of course, our good friends, the local druggists — first Marshall Nicholson and later, George Austin.

These two men were very good to my dad, and I will always count them as special friends. Dad wanted no sympathy. I know that he lived his life to the fullest and made up his mind early that, although he knew his sickness was there, he just was not going to pay much attention to it. His disease was not accompanied by pain, and I am sure that that helped. All during our growing up, I don't think that we kids ever really paid much attention to this, simply because Dad never said a thing. I can remember the water boiling on the stove for the hypodermic needle, but such things did not register that much.

The one thing I remember well about my dad was that he was a vital man. He was always ready to enjoy life to its fullest. He, like my mother, loved people, but he was not demonstrative like Mother was, except with her. He never got close to Mother that he did not touch her or put his arms around her or show her some kind of affection — always. Many times in the evening they would take long walks together, hand in hand, like a pair of teenage lovers. They were very much in love, and that love grew stronger and stronger as the years wore on.

Dad was very interested in the out-of-doors, and we went there at the drop of a hat. I can only remember a few Sundays that we didn't go somewhere after church. We explored every side road and every mountain road the car could go over, and we went everywhere imaginable in the state. This urge to explore and to know stayed with all of us, and our traveling gave us an appreciation of the history and geography of the state that few people today can boast. I guess we went into every nook and cranny of this beautiful state. As we rode along, Dad would tell us about the history of the area, the wildflowers, the grass, the trees — you name it. It was not only fun, it was educational. Dad just naturally made a study of these things. He collected all kinds of books on the history of the area. He became quite a photographer, taking remarkable and beautiful pictures of the mountains and valleys wherever we were. His pictures of wildflowers are classic, and they are used, even now, in the study of plant life of the area.

Dad's interests were varied, and he was thorough in his understanding of the things that interested him. He was also concerned for our country, our state, and the immediate area around him, and he never turned down an opportunity to serve somewhere for the betterment of same.

You know, they always say that many people are never fully appreciated until they're gone. This has become more and more of a truism as the years have gone by. Not that Dad was not appreciated or well liked by everyone during his life, because he was. But since Dad has been gone and I have gone through another seventeen years of life, I am constantly finding out more and more about the good and unselfish things that he did to make an easier and better life for other people. One of the girls I grew up with told me just recently that if it had not been for my dad, they would surely have starved. When she lost her father, my dad stepped in and saw to it that the family received food, money, and whatever few benefits they could receive in the Depression days. Another man, quite prominent here in Arizona, told me that he had gone to school with my dad in the years we were in Glendale, and he said that no one, not even his own father, had ever influenced him as my dad did. I could go on and on with story after story of my dad's unselfish devotion to his fellowman. But he wanted no recognition, no glory — that wasn't his way. He did these things out of his compassion for others. Probably the finest tribute anyone can ever have, and very few ever achieve, was paid to Dad after he had passed away. One of his old, close friends came up to me at the cemetery and said, "Bob, I never knew a person, nor did I ever hear of a person, who ever had a bad word to say about your dad." He was loved by everyone with whom he came in touch. He was a man who, because of his own problems, could have felt sorry for himself and waited for others to serve him, to take care of him; but that wasn't my dad.

Growing up in my home was, by and large, a fun time. We were always on the go. We kids were always involved in all kinds of things. I was playing all kinds of sports, working in grocery stores, playing for dances, and so on. Carol, my younger sister, was already making her own clothes when she was in the fourth grade. She learned the piano from Mother, and she was a cute girl with all kinds of personality. She got that, I'm sure, from Mother. Dick, my younger brother, was a very quiet little boy who you really did not even know was around, he was so quiet. But we three enjoyed each other and had a good time with one another, as far as older brother and younger ones can get along. Carol was always in my hair as we got older. She wanted, as any younger member of the family, to be where the action was. Well, this meant to tag along after me, and, man, I just didn't want her. And I know that when I was in high school and later in college, Carol had a "crush" on every one of my friends at one time or another. You know how those things are. When I was doing my "thing" and with my crowd, I sure did not want a younger sister around. She could be a pest this way. Of course, she went crying to Dad or Mother about my mistreating her, and they would smooth it over, usually by appealing to me to be nicer to her, or some such nonsense. She was really a weight around my neck when she got to the eighth grade. They held that class in the high school building, so Carol had to walk with me to school. What big grown-up teenager and "big wheel on campus" wanted his little sister tagging along? Not me! But there she would come behind me, as fast as her little legs would go, and I would walk as fast as I could to get away from her. But I don't think I've described anything original — this goes on in every family I ever heard of. Looking back, I've realized that this little girl had a hero and I was he, but I certainly didn't want any of it at the time. And this is also true of most families. Dick was so much younger, some nine years, that he was just the "little brother." Dick had been a very sick little boy the early years of his life, and we almost lost him several times with pneumonia and the complications of it. I think this had a lot to do with his quiet way.

Oh, sure, the younger ones were "pains," but there was still a sharing and caring among us all. We were all very close, and I can remember many a day that I did all kinds of activities with the younger ones.

All in all, it was family life that you would not have really expected in a small, dusty, western town in the Depression, but it existed and it was good.

I go back to my Dad, again, because I realize what a leader of the family he was, in his quiet way. I have told something of his burdens and of the sicknesses and problems that he and Mother had, but don't feel sorry for them. They lived a good life, and they enjoyed life in all its ramifications.

They always say the "good die young." That was never truer than in the case of my parents. Dad was only sixty when he went, a victim of years of struggle with that dread disease he carried in his body. When my mother died, I thought that Dad just could not take it. And, you know, he never let the memories of Mother and his love for her dim in any way. Even though gone, she remained the focal point of his life until he went. Now, don't get me wrong that he lived in some sort of morbid grief. That I do not mean. He lived with his memories his last few years, but as always, he lived a good life. He took photographs; he left the experimental farm in Safford to return to Willcox and start a new life. He built a beautiful home with enough room so that we kids and our own families had plenty of room to visit him, and he did as always — he served his fellowman. Sure, there were some single ladies who set their cap for him, and we kids, in a very generous and, we thought, well-intentioned move, suggested that he might remarry if he found someone he could be comfortable with. That was the wrong thing to say — Dad blew up! I mean, he really came unglued and informed us that "he would lead his own life and that he was not about to settle for second-best." So, that took care of that.

I could go on and on about the family, and especially our parents, but I would never get further. This was and always will be a favorite subject of mine. I guess it takes maturity and going through some of the trauma and trials of raising your own family before you can fully appreciate what your parents were and what they did. Yes, I feel that my dad and mother were two very special people, head and shoulders above the crowd. I just know that the good Lord took them early in life because they were such good and wonderful people that he had to have them with Him, just to be there and help out. And I know that that is what they are doing right now.

Uncle Dick

BACK IN THOSE DAYS, our valley and mountains possessed a real status symbol of that particular time, dude ranches. These were ranches that had become the resorts of that era, the only difference being that you paid to stay at the ranch and to work on it, also. Most were, as they say, "working dude ranches." Some of the ranchers who enjoyed herding tenderfeet as well as cattle had, over the years, turned their places into fancy hostelries with horses and cows. Rich people from the East came in droves to see the "Wild West" and to actually live on a ranch. I'm sure the tales they told when they returned home were pretty far out, because the old cowboys on those places really told some whoppers. After all, we had to live up to our reputation.

These ranches got to be well-known and very popular around the country, and one of the most popular and best-known of all in that area was the 76. The 76 was governed by one of the most remarkable characters of the entire West, Mrs. Clare Webb. I am not going to tell you her life history yet, but you just have to know more about her. Her 76 Ranch was located in the foothills of the Graham Mountains and not far from the Bonita schoolhouse I told about previously. It was a pretty place in the rolling hills with juniper, oak, scrub pine, manzanita, and other mountain shrubbery all around. The main ranch building was surrounded by scattered cabins, barns, corrals, and other outbuildings. All of these buildings were built of stuccoed adobe and, as I remember, of a rather pinkish hue, which, believe it or not, did not take away from their attractiveness.

Into this setting, one day in the early thirties, came a man in a Model A Ford pickup piled high with all the possessions he owned, evidently. He could have been young, old, or middle-aged; it was impossible to tell, with his beard and all. He came into the main ranch building to ask Mrs. Webb for the opportunity to rent an old line cabin, back up a side canyon and further up the mountain from the main ranch headquarters. It seemed that this old boy had pretty well scouted out this cabin, because he knew all about it: that it was deserted, that it had a spring nearby, and other facts. Mrs. Webb was flabbergasted to think that anybody in their right mind would want to live in that old shack and rent it, to boot. But she was pretty shrewd and a darned good judge of character, and somehow she liked this fellow. A lot of us in her place, I know, would probably have run him off, but not her. She just knew that he was all right; if he wanted to live there and pay rent for that place, he might not be too bright, but he was all right! So she agreed to the request.

He told her that his name was Dick Calkins, that this was one of the prettiest places he had ever seen, and that he sure knew he was going to be happy up there. He vowed to make the place into a showplace. Mrs. Webb had her doubts about that, but it was up to him.

Dick moved in, and it wasn't long before he began to show up in town, usually every Saturday. Saturday was the big day in town. Everyone was out. The ranchers, farmers, cowboys, farm hands, and townspeople (so as not to miss any excitement) all mingled on the sidewalks and in the grocery stores and saloons. It was always a great day. As I look back on it, it was like one great big reception, cocktail party, Sunday School picnic, political convention, and family get-together, lumped into one day. It was a day to greet friends you saw once a week, do the shopping, mailing, banking, whatever. There was always a good crowd at the White Palace, playing pool and doing some drinking. And the same at Rix's. The cafes were busy; the slot machines that lined the walls of the cafes and bars were whirring constantly. It was a fun time. The streets were crowded with cars and trucks. The ranchers who had money drove pickups and Lincoln Continentals, and there were a bunch of them. Over at the city park there was always something going on. The kids turned it into a football or baseball field, or just had good old wrestling matches, and there was always some Bible-yelling soul who could give out with the Scriptures and a good hell-fire and damnation sermon under a tree. There were also various and sundry types who had all kinds of trinkets or gadgets to sell, and often old Joe Clark would be lying out there on the grass with a couple of boards leading up and over his chest, all the kids riding bicycles over him — he was *strong.*

At night, all the "decent" folks went home, or they went home to change clothes, eat, and get ready for the big dance, because there was always a dance in Willcox. Either it was held at the Women's Club building, at one of the bars, out at a roadhouse called Mexico Way, or (which hardly ever happened) you had to go out to one of the rural schoolhouses. But Saturday night was a time for kicking up your heels.

Well, back to "Uncle" Dick — that's what people began to call him, especially the kids. He came to town in his Model A on Saturday and went to the post office to mail a package, oblong and crudely wrapped in regular wrapping paper. Then it was off to greet the people of Willcox and to do his weekly "layin' in." In other words, getting his supplies. Most of the populace paid very little attention to Dick and his activities. Everyone liked him, but we all just thought he was some type of eccentric living off there in the mountains in that old-line cabin. Now, mind you, no one considered him to be a hermit or something like that — he was too nice and he was friendly to all.

Dick Calkins lived his life and the rest of the valley lived theirs, and I don't believe that anyone ever gave much thought about the package Dick mailed or anything else he did. He was just one of the Saturday "come-to-towners."

Well, the war came on, and all my buddies and I left for parts unknown. By that time we all had gotten to know him and liked him as he liked us. After we all returned from the service, we saw Dick from time to time, but things hadn't changed, and he was just part of the scenery. Then we all got the surprise of our lives. Most of my friends and I were off at the University of Arizona when we found that Uncle Dick had purchased a ranch over in the Galiuro Mountains, across the valley from where he had spent all those many years. It was a big question in everyone's mind as to where a man like him would get the money to buy anything, much less a ranch. All of those years, Dick was certainly not known to have a lot of money, and the amount of his weekly purchases certainly bore that out. But here he was, a rancher.

As we wondered and questioned, the truth finally came out. Many things came to light and, to our further amazement, we found that we had had a celebrity right there in our midst and hadn't known it. It turned out that the oblong package he mailed regularly was on its way to the nation's newspapers, because what our good Dick Calkins was doing all those years up in the mountains was drawing the very famous cartoon of "Buck Rogers." For the younger set who might be reading this, "Buck Rogers" was the most famous and original cartoon depicting travel and life in outer space and on other planets.

Dick turned the cartoon over to a syndicate and retired from active cartooning. True to his nature, he began devoting his time to the wayward boys at Fort Grant (the Industrial School for Boys), close to his former residence at the 76 Ranch. He volunteered to teach them arts and crafts and painting. Of course, his efforts were well-received, since it was not often that anyone had a chance to learn from a man like him.

He named his ranch "The Buckskin," and he fixed up the ranch headquarters. His wife soon appeared on the scene. Now, I had heard rumors that there were a wife and family, but I was never sure until she actually came along. I understood that there was also a son, but I never did see him.

For many years, Dick gave of his time and his talent. In the meantime, the "space race" began, and do you know what happened? The space boys took a long look at some of Dick's cartoons and began to design space suits and other apparatus from the cartoon. They began to operate in space along the lines that

Dick had already thought of. It was inevitable that the astronauts began to write and to communicate with Dick, to recognize him for the space pioneer that he was. In his time, Dick Calkins the rancher and volunteer helper at a boys' school saw his cartoon ideas brought to reality. He had never doubted for a minute that this would happen, and perhaps this explains why he led the life he did. Was it solitude that enabled him to think about these things, or was he afraid he might be ridiculed for actually thinking that such space travel and other miraculous things that took place would actually happen? That question has never been answered.

The original seven astronauts became good friends of Dick, through letters and telephone conversations. I know it was a gratifying experience for this kind man, who was now, in the early sixties, beginning to grow old, or at least older than we had ever thought throughout those early years of his residence in the mountains and the valley he adopted as his home.

When Dick died, he was buried in Tucson. He left a small part of the ranch and a small ranch house to his wife for as long as she might want it. This, too, added more mystery to the reason for his living as he did.

Whatever the reason or purpose, Dick Calkins left his mark on the valley and on the world and added another exciting and somewhat mysterious chapter to the history of the valley.

Cattle Capital of the World

We locals of Willcox were very impressed with the fact that our little town bore the title of Cattle Capital of the World. That may sound like a grandiose title, but to a certain extent, it was true. We were actually the locality shipping the most cattle "right off the range" in the United States and, very possibly, in the world. In those days, with the exception of a few dry-land farms, the Willcox area was strictly cattle country. We were right in the center of the big ranch country. The ranches, in those days, were measured in terms of "sections." No one mentioned acres, it was always sections. It took a lot of ground to pasture very many cattle, but in those days the average ranch was just plain big. A section consisted of 640 acres, or one square mile, so when we talk about the "spreads" in those days, we are talking about a lot of land.

I knew all the ranchers around us for miles, and I mean for miles. They came to town to do their business, especially on Saturday, and they participated in the social life of the town. They were, for the most part, plain, everyday, good people. Many of them maintained homes in town simply because the wife did not want any part of the loneliness and seclusion of the ranch, or because they had kids who had to go to school. In those days, the ranches were spaced far and wide, and the ranchers had to see to it themselves that their children got to town to school. There were a number of rural grade schools that took care of a number of ranch children, but there were no other high schools available except in our town and other small towns scattered in the valley. In high school, the children of the town and the ranch kids grew up together.

The ranch people got the red carpet treatment whenever they came to town, because the townspeople depended on them for their living. The whole area had one product — cattle.

I mentioned in a previous chapter about the large holding pens along the railroad just out of town on the north side. Twice each year, in spring and fall, the ranchers drove their cows to this siding, oftentimes for many miles. From there they would ship their cattle to the markets, mainly to the Midwest. It was a sight to see: the big herds coming into the pens and the thousands of cows being readied for shipment. For weeks at a time we would go to bed to the sounds of bawling cattle just outside of town. The funny thing is that I never once heard a complaint about all the noise, and it was indeed noisy. We townspeople knew where our bread and butter came from. We town kids would go down to the pens and watch the men load the cows into the cars and watch the cowboys herding them along. It is a shame that people of this day and time cannot see and know this sight. It's all history now, since the beef cow off the range is marketed altogether differently. But this whole operation was a real part of Americana. Each year fifty to eighty thousand head were sent to market from Willcox.

The typical rancher in that area was a man ranging in age from his forties to his sixties, although there were a number that were older. He was either a pioneer who had settled his own spread, or he was a second-generation cowman who was carrying on the family ranch. These men were *"all"* men. They were tough and hard when necessary, but most were true gentlemen. These ranchers were the epitome of what we think of as the real rancher — tough, rugged, gentle with his women, rough with his enemies, independent, and, really, the "good guy with the white hat." This is the way they were. I don't believe that statement would be very true today, but then it was. Oh, sure, some of those old boys were pretty salty and wild, and some you had better watch your dealings with, because they could get to you pretty quick. But, in all honesty, I say that the rancher in Willcox of my time was a "good guy."

One had to admire these people. They lived a hard, solitary, and sometimes very lonely life out in their remote ranches. But they loved it. They loved the land; it was theirs. They fought for it in many instances, and they fought the droughts, they fought disease, they built fence, they did whatever it took. And they were an independent lot — they wanted help from no one. Even today, the cowman is one of the very few people who has never accepted help or subsidy of any kind from the government, or anyone else for that matter.

The cowman was king, and he knew it, but most wore their mantle well. They knew that they were the hub of everything, but they did not use their economic power over the people of the towns. If they did, I don't remember it.

As you might suspect, these ranchers and their cowboys came to town to take care of the necessities — to buy their supplies, get a haircut and a shave (that was a real luxury, because some of them hit town looking pretty raunchy). They came to go to the bank, to go to the feed store to lay in a supply of feed and salt to use as they needed. Most importantly, many came to get to their favorite "watering hole" or to hit one of the pool halls and get in some games. Most of the ranchers had their wives along, so their drinking and playing activities were pretty curtailed, but the cowboys came to have a good time, and their good time started early in the day. After all, they'd been out there riding the range, eating

31

dust, and working usually from sunup to sundown, and they were ready to play. And play they did.

Ranches of any size, and most were pretty good size, had their cowhands in those days. All the work was done by hand; all the new gadgets and new methods we hear of today were just not around. A good cowboy in those days made a few dollars a month and got his room and board. You could go out to any of the ranches and see these men working, doing jobs like you see in the Western movies and on television. Movies sometimes glamorize these jobs, however. But branding, midwifing cows, fixing fence, hauling water and feed, cleaning corrals, keeping up the tack and the gear, and a thousand other dirty and tough jobs just are not my idea of glamour. But these cowboys had been doing such work since they were kids, and although they might grumble and groan, the work had a hold on them that made them keep on. There wasn't any money in it, and there sure wasn't any future for these men, but the "hold" was there. About the only things they could look forward to were their weekly trips to town. And, many times, they might not make that but every other week, depending on the work to be done. So they came to town to play hard, just like they had to work hard.

The guy who owned the ranch, the rancher himself, by and large presented a different image. Not that some of them didn't play hard, too. They did, but for the most part they conducted themselves well. All who I knew, and I knew just about all of them around our part of the country, had that same look about them. No matter what their physique, they looked "outdoorsy." They had on the usual outfits, including their favorite Stetson. Contrary to popular notion, these were not the large, ten-gallon variety, usually. They were smaller, stylized hats that suited their wearer. When ranchers took their hats off, you could see where their tan, weatherbeaten face left off and the white of the top of their forehead and their hairline began. This line came from being out in the sun. They wore a western-style shirt, Levi's with a leather belt and a buckle, and good-looking, expensive boots. The boots, the belt and buckle, and the hat were the cowman's pride and joy, and he spent whatever he could to have the best. When he dressed up for a dance, some of those western shirts and suits and all the rest added up to a pretty penny. As for the cowboy, he might be wearing all of his material wealth right on his back.

Many of these ranchers were of pioneer stock, and their history went back to the early days of the area. You could go east up through Dos Cabezas and get into the Riggs settlement. This whole area is nestled in a pocket bounded on the west by the Dos Cabezas and on the north and east by the Chiricahuas. This was prime ranchland, and it sure seemed so to Brannick Riggs and his family when they first hit this country in the middle 1800s. Brannick got in with the

Cattle drive, outside Willcox (COURTESY "ARIZONA RANGE NEWS," WILLCOX)

cavalry there at Fort Bowie and did some scouting for them, spending most of his early and middle life fighting with and working with the Apache. When you get down the road about halfway into their land, you can turn north and go right into Apache Pass and right up to the old fort. So I guess it was just natural that Brannick and his family got tied in with the Army in those days. So it was with Neal Erickson, who was a bona fide Army scout. Many years later, as a senior in high school, I participated in Neal's funeral. As you take the road into the Wonderland of Rocks, the fantastic national monument to the north of the Riggs family ranchhouses, you start into the mountains. Just as you hit the first foot-hills, you can see a small cemetery to your right as you go in. We buried Neal there alongside his wife in the most impressive ceremony I have ever seen. It was a military ceremony. At the end, I began "taps" on my bugle, and as the sound began to fade away, another bugler at the base of the mountain began; as his last notes faded away, a bugler clear on the other side of the mountain completed the echoing effect. It was impressive, and those mournful sounds echoed and reechoed around and across the mountains, a final tribute to a great pioneer and a courageous man.

The Riggs settlement, as it had always been known, is populated by the Riggs families and the Stark families, although not many Starks are left in that area. Some of these families are cousins, uncles, sons, daughters, and so on, and, in time, there have been some other names added to the area as marriages occurred. And there were always a few "outsiders" who owned land in and around the settlement proper. As is prevalent among these families, there is a large family cemetery not far off the main road through the settlement. Generations of the Riggs' families have been laid to rest there. Most of the families were the descendants of John and B. K. Riggs.

I certainly cannot forget the ladies. I sometimes feel that these ranchwomen were really the backbone of the whole ranch operation. They lived in remote houses, raising the families without very much in the way of conveniences, and they gave moral support to their men. If called on, most of them could get out and work with the cattle right alongside their men.

I can remember one beautiful lady who, though blind, ran a ranch for many, many years. Now that is a feat that cannot be topped. She rode her horse and did all types of chores — a very remarkable person.

These ranch women also gave their children religious teaching and, oftentimes, the basic three "R's," if the closest school happened to be too far away. They were a hardy lot, but they were very pretty, almost without exception. They came to town dressed up because it was an occasion, they were tan from the hours in the sun, and they were in every way *ladies*. As I said, the children got much of their early education from their parents, if the nearest schoolhouse was too far away, but most did get to these one-room schools. They were situated all over the valley. As they reached high school age, these boys and girls were brought to town to live in boardinghouses or with some of the town families, because it was just too far to bring them into town every day.

As has been the trend, most of this generation did not return to ranch life. Of course, this was not very possible, in many cases, because many of them were children of the ranch foremen or managers. So there just wasn't a family ranch to go to. I do know, also, that many of them wanted no part of the hard life they had grown up in. All of these boys and girls, in my day, were good and close friends. Something about them, patterned after their folks, gave them a special quality.

It may sound like I have idealized the rancher and the cowboy. I mean to do just that. I admired them. They were just as I have said. Oh, sure, there were some that I could have done without, and there were some "rounders" among them. There were the older people. You can imagine that history was right there with us when you realize that a rancher in his fifties and sixties had been around when the old gunfighters and the Indians were running loose in the area. Also, you had to remember that many of these men were rough and tough if needs be, and you surely did not want to cross them in any way. Many of these men had come into this land as young men, and you just did not question where they came from and under what circumstances, because you might be surprised at what you turned up. Some of the old-timers had lived a past that just did not fit in with the life they were living now. But let me state that, whatever the circumstances of their arrival in the valley many years before, these were still good men. As I said before, these ranchers were the pioneers that came to the valley and started their own spread as young men. A few were second-generation valley-ites, but not many.

It's funny, in a way, but I just don't remember that a lot of fuss was made over ranch life at the time. I guess it was just a fact of life, like living in a mining town or any other one-industry town. We accepted the fact that this was what made the area go, and the ranchers were just our everyday friends and neighbors, "no big deal." Of course, now that I look back on it, I realize that it *was* a big deal. My family and I took rides many Sunday afternoons, visiting our friends among the ranchers. Those were fun times. It was big ranch country, the countryside was beautiful, the people were friendly and happy to see us. There was always food and a lot of talk, mainly reminiscing. These people loved to talk about the past. Well, the past hadn't been too far away. And the stories we would hear!

I can remember going up to the Finley Ranch in the Dragoons, the mountains directly south of Willcox where Cochise Stronghold is located. To get to Finleys', you went down through the Dry Lake, through the little village of Cochise, climbed up into the Texas Canyon area, through the little village of Dragoon, and on south to the ranch. The Finleys had two boys about my age, which always led to a lot of fun. I can remember the ranch house, a large, rambling, wooden affair with a funny-looking little tower on the roof, where members of the family went to keep lookout for Indians back in the days when the Apache was right around close. In fact, many Apaches were right across the mountain. If Indians were sighted, the family quickly beat a retreat to a stone blockhouse up on a small hill near the house. This was provisioned with food and water, and there were the usual holes all around to fire rifles from. We kids had many an imaginary Indian raid and fight out there every time we visited.

Directly north of town, out through the Stewart district (then a small, sparsely settled farming area) and out toward Bonita and Fort Grant, was the big cienega country. A cienega is a low, marshy, swampy area where water, either through some form of artesian action or through the surfacing of a small stream, pools up, giving a nice water supply. This was prime ranch land, too. This part of the valley was surrounded by the Winchesters and the Galiuros to the west, the Grahams to the north, and the smaller hills of the Circle I's and Dos Cabezas to the east. This was Hooker land, by and large.

The Hookers' Sierra Bonita Ranch was something to see. It covered most of that area and held a number of cienegas. The ranch house, which still stands much as it did then, is nestled in a huge cottonwood grove. The house was built around a huge patio, forming a square. The dining room could seat approximately one hundred people. Colonel Clay Hooker, the founder of the ranch, had come to Fort Grant in the Indian days. He left the Army after the Civil War and came to this area to raise turkeys, later to start this ranch. The Colonel surrounded himself with ranch hands — about one hundred of them — and, by some strange coincidence, they were pretty good gun-hands. In other words, the man had his own army, so they say. Perhaps, because of his Army life and because of his location, he might have been afraid of Indian raids or the like. Indian raids surely were a menace, but I've heard many an old-timer say that the good Colonel had a lot of different ideas for his men. Whatever the original purpose, I never did hear of them riding out en masse and doing anything they shouldn't. But it was well-known in those days that the Hooker ranch was well-protected. The Indians knew it, too, and with its proximity to the Fort, the ranch was not a favorite target for the "Apach'."

In my day, I knew Harry Hooker, Jessie, and their daughter, Rinki. Harry was the old Colonel's grandson, and he had inherited much of the old Colonel's bearing. Harry was a tough, hard, but efficient rancher. He was about as independent as they come. Jessie, his wife, was the same way, and when Harry passed away, she took hold of the reins and ran the ranch, no doubt about that!

The Colonel was a good friend of Wyatt Earp. Wyatt was on his way to visit the ranch when he and Curly Bill Brocius confronted each other at Sulphur Springs, down the valley. The legendary gunfight occurred and, according to Wyatt, he killed Curly Bill and left him there at the springs. But no one ever found his body. When this happened, Earp did not continue to the Sierra Bonita Ranch, but turned back to Tombstone to inform the populace of the event. Nevertheless, these two men, Earp and Hooker, had formed a bond of friendship of some sort and on some common ground. (Others have written that this event occurred elsewhere, but I always heard from the old-timers that the Sulphur Springs was the scene.)

The Sierra Bonita Ranch goes on. Both Harry and Jessie are gone, but Rinki and her son continue. I cannot go by the area and see that big grove of trees sitting out there in the valley close to the mountains and not be fascinated by the setting and the history of the ranch.

There is so much history behind many of these ranches and the ranchers that I could go on and on about them. The ranchers were fascinating people, and they all had stories to tell. I spent many a Sunday afternoon out visiting, along with my folks, listening (with mouth wide open) at the yarns that were spun.

I certainly must mention the women who ran their own spreads. I've told you about Lillian Riggs, whose blindness did not deter her one bit; she ran that ranch as well as any man with two good eyes. I've also mentioned Mrs. Webb and the 76 Ranch. It was funny but true that many of the dude ranches in the area in my time were run by women.

Early in the 1900s, W. T. Webb had established the 76 Ranch, not too far from the Sierra Bonita Ranch. Well, W. T. had some business in New York City, way back there, and he left for a routine trip. While there, he attended the Ziegfield Follies and fell for a "pair of legs" in the chorus line. He decided to court this pretty young thing, and he married her and brought her out to the wilds of Arizona. She had been one of the original "Flora-dora" girls in the Follies and was a good-looking woman. I've heard her talk many times about her early days on the ranch. She didn't know what to expect and was scared of everything. She told me many times that she thought she would never get used to the strange sounds of the coyotes, a mountain lion screaming once in a while, the snakes, and, mainly, the hard life. But she had determined to stick it out, and she survived. Well, Mr. Webb died and left his wife, this "concrete canyon" product, out there in the wilderness, to go it alone. I'm sure that there were many people who just knew she would pack up and shake the dust of Arizona pretty quick, but she fooled 'em, and I think she fooled herself. She took over the ranch and then, probably because she loved entertaining and having a lot of people around, she turned the ranch into a dude operation. As I said before, these were working ranches where people from the Middle West, the East, and so on, paid good money to come and spend their vacations working the ranch. Boy, you don't find that kind of deal going on these days. These days it's tough enough to get anyone to work on purpose, much less pay money to work — and ranching isn't my idea of a vacation. Back then, however, this was the "la-de-da" thing to do. These "dudes" were wealthy people. Anyway, Mrs. Webb saw a good thing and cashed in on it. During her banner days, she counted the rich and the famous as guests at the ranch. Her business flourished and she ran that place better, I'm sure, than did her late husband.

Talk about the rich and the famous, I can remember one night when we played for a dance out at the Bonita schoolhouse. There was a couple who were having a good time, but the strange thing was that they seemed to be pretty "lovey-dovey," although the man was up there in years and the lady was young. There was a real difference in age, but they were having a good time. They would come over and request this piece and that one, and we obliged them. When the dance was over we found that this was a honeymooning couple, the Stokowskis — Leopold and his wife, the former Gloria Vanderbilt. Mrs. Webb was always full of surprises!

Over in back of the Winchesters was another well-known dude ranch, the Muleshoe. It was run by another lady, Mrs. MacMurray. There were also the Silver Spur, the Triangle T, and others. The Triangle T sits right in the middle of Texas Canyon, a very picturesque canyon in the Dragoons. The highway passes through this area, and it is very scenic with all kinds of rock formations. Travelers coming in from either side are always surprised at seeing all this. As you go through now, if you look to the east as you near the Dragoon exit, you will see a funny-looking little wooden shelter sitting on the rocks. Back in World War II, the U.S. Government housed, or interned, the Japanese Embassy people at the Triangle T Ranch. These little shelters among the rocks were for the guards to sit in and keep watch on the Japanese Embassy people as they went about their daily routine.

I know the rancher and his family who have to have been the family that was written about in "High Chaparral," the television series. Now, of course, I don't have any idea that that ever happened, but I never did see "High Chaparral" that I didn't think about one of our well-known ranchers. All the circumstances, the way they lived — everything was a complete duplicate of this particular family.

I could go on and on. As you can tell, I was taken with the ranch people — still am, for that matter. Probably the main reason I have always admired and respected these people is because, even today, they are still the pioneers, the example of what America is all about. They work hard, play hard, rely on themselves. They ask for no help, especially from the government — and their lot has been hard, especially lately. They live out on their land, with an extreme love for it, and their word is their bond. Sound idealistic? You bet. Isn't it a shame that the rest of our country cannot take a lesson from the rancher? We sure wouldn't be in the fix we are now if it did.

Meet the Old Lady

As I LOOK BACK on those years, it was amazing that so many unusual and different experiences happened to me. If I were to go back through Willcox now and mention these things to most of the residents there now, I would only succeed in flabbergasting them. Or, worse yet, they'd probably think that I am just a great storyteller — accent on "story."

I'm sure that not much happens down that way anymore. If it does, I sure don't hear about it. Now, I'm not saying that only when I lived there did all the action occur, but it sure seems so!

This little episode is a sequel to my chapter on the ranchers. As I've said, Mrs. Webb of the 76 Ranch was a real character and full of surprises. All the town knew her, admired her, respected her, and, you better believe, catered to her. What Mrs. Webb wanted in town, she usually got, no questions asked. She pumped a lot of money into that little town. She did big business with those dudes out at the ranch.

Back then, we had passenger trains coming through that stopped in Willcox. Just about every stop produced Eastern visitors, come out to spend their money and their vacation working on a ranch. There was always someone in town from one or a number of the dude spreads to pick up their guests.

I returned to Willcox from my stint in the Navy in May of 1946. My only ambition that summer was to take it easy, play some softball in the summer league, maybe do a little traveling around to see some of my good friends. Then, in the fall, I would head back to the University of Arizona. I didn't have plans to work hard, or work at all. Well, the best laid plans.... Marshall Nicholson, owner of the drug store, asked me to work for him until I went back to school. I helped move the store from its original location over on Railroad Avenue, across from the little city park, to the old Rottman building on the corner of Haskell and Maley. Haskell is the main drag. I've told you how highly I thought of Marshall Nicholson; there was just no way I would turn him down. So I became an employee of the Nicholson Drugstore, reluctantly at first, but then it became a lot of fun. In fact, I cannot remember a more fun time than that summer, working with Marshall, with his great grin and funny chuckle, and

George Austin, the druggist (now the owner of the store), who was a real joker. You had to watch yourself with George — he was liable to pull anything. Mae Moore also worked there, a real lady with a great personality all her own. I couldn't have found a better bunch. We had fun, but we worked hard — had to, being the only drugstore in town.

I reported for work down at the old store and we started moving. What a chore, and what discoveries we made. That old store had been in the same location since the late 1800s. We found old bottles of tincture of orange peel and bottles full of herbs, leaves of whatever kind, and you name it. I wish I had some of those old bottles now, they're worth a fortune.

The new store had large windows, from near the floor to the ceiling, all around. Nothing would do except that the prescription counter and the whole drug area be built just inside one of those huge windows. George was doing most of the prescription filling, and he wanted to be able to stand there and look out on the main street and watch the action. With that in mind, Marshall asked me if I had ever built any shelves or done much carpentry. I sure hadn't. It made no difference, though, because I was designated "resident carpenter," and George and I built those shelves and the prescription counter. To my amazement, we did a pretty decent job. In fact, those shelves stayed right there for twenty years or so. I can still see George, shaking up some sort of concoction, standing inside the window and watching the traffic go by. Those mixtures must have still been all right, since I didn't hear any complaints.

To digress a bit, when this carpentry work was done, we settled down into a regular business routine. I soon learned a great deal about the products sold in a drugstore. I hadn't realized how soon I would become an ersatz doctor. People felt that since I was in the drugstore, I could make recommendations on all kinds of ailments. Don't believe for a minute that I was running around in there prescribing or anything. But I could recommend and discuss remedies with customers, as long as they were regular patented medicines right off the shelf. I had good teachers. Mae even clued me in on ladies' cosmetics.

The biggest and most revealing surprise to me was that I became knowledgeable on people's sex lives. In those days, pills and other types of birth control devices were not around, so people went to the local druggist for whatever was available. I soon found out that there was a lot going on in that little town. Until that point I hadn't been aware of the tremendous popularity of sex. Some of the customers were very surprising. Many of them weren't married, and even those that were, we were pretty sure that some of their purchases were made for use somewhere else. I could write another book on this subject, but I don't dare.

Meet the Old Lady

The summer wore on, and I spent my days down at the store and nearly every evening playing softball in our summer league. George was pulling practical jokes on everyone, Mae was working hard and was fun to be around, and Marshall was his usual self — jovial, knowledgeable, as close to being the town doctor as the doctor himself. He had been ministering to everyone's particular ills for a long time, and everybody trusted him.

Our work routine had everyone but me going to lunch at the usual time. I would stay on from twelve to one and hold down the store. Then at one I usually went home for lunch. Mother would always have something good. One day in August when I was in the store by myself, the phone rang. It was Mrs. Webb out at the 76 Ranch. She asked, "Bob, what're you doing?" I replied, "Working, what do you think?" She went on, "Bob, I have a guest coming in from the East on the train, an old lady. I can't get in town until about half past four or five o'clock. Would you do me a favor?" I said I would. She said that she wanted me to meet this lady and take her over to the Willcox Hotel, where she had arranged for a room for her to freshen up. Then she would be in to get her. I asked her how I would know or recognize her. Mrs. Webb replied, "Oh, just go over there — she'll be the only one getting off. Nobody else will be getting off in Willcox." She hung up. When Marshall returned, I told him about the conversation, and he said, "Sure, get over there about 2:25 and meet the train for her." I went home, got a bite to eat, returned, and at the appointed time I wandered over to the train station. It was only a block away. The station agent was outside and had a baggage cart with some shipments ready to go out. He was agent, porter, freight agent, janitor, and everything else. "You meeting somebody?" he asked. I told him that I was Mrs. Webb's greeter for one of her guests.

Sure enough, the train came right on time. Southern Pacific's pride and joy was this passenger train. We had two passenger trains stopping in Willcox in those days, two from each direction. In the wintertime, quite a few people got off to go to the dude ranches, but in the summertime, this tapered off to nothing. When the train stopped, only the agent and I were out there. He put his baggage on, and I waited for somebody to get off. Nothing happened for a few minutes. Then, near the rear of the train, there was some commotion. People got off, and the conductor was off, so I walked slowly back that way. When I got closer I could see a rather large, older lady, walking with a decided limp. Right then and there, I could have "shot" Mrs. Webb. There was no difficulty in recognizing the "old lady," as she had described her. I was a one-man greeting committee for Mrs. Eleanor Roosevelt. You can imagine my feelings — I sure wasn't prepared for this!

I mustered up my courage and my best manners and approached this fine lady. She was very gracious. I told her that we were just going right across the street, that a room had been reserved for her there, and that Mrs. Webb would be in later. We made small talk on the way across the street. The station agent and I carried her luggage. He had not said one word all the way; he was still in shock. When we got inside the hotel, Paul Duncan, one of the owners, took care of all the amenities. I was ready to leave and go back to work when Mrs. Roosevelt asked, "Young man, where are you going?" I replied that I had to return to work at the drugstore. She stated that she was not about to stay at the hotel and asked if she could go with me. I assured her that she could. I was delighted. The word spread quickly that she was there, and we could see people peeking out of store windows as we went by. Marshall took everything right in stride and, as soon as we got to the store, he got out his favorite old overstuffed easy chair for Mrs. Roosevelt. She told us to just go about our business — that she would be fine right there. We placed her chair in an area of the store where she could see everything going on. We got her a cold drink, and for the rest of the afternoon she held forth from her chair. She visited with us and all of the people who came in, and she seemed to have a great time. We thoroughly enjoyed her. Finally Mrs. Webb arrived, and they departed for the ranch. Meeting Mrs. Roosevelt was quite an experience, and one I shall never forget.

As a footnote to this, I might add that Mrs. Webb and the entire Roosevelt family were very close friends. Were you to see the pictures of the inaugurations of Franklin D. Roosevelt, you would see Mrs. Webb right there in the box with the family. Mrs. Webb had pictures of these and other occasions with the Roosevelts hanging on the walls of the ranch house. Further amazement is due when you realize that Mrs. Webb was an ardent and active Republican — in fact, a Republican committee-woman from Arizona.

"Go meet the old lady on the train" — isn't that a kicker!

Tall Men-Tall Tales

WYATT EARP, Doc Holliday, Johnny Ringo, Curly Bill — they all lived here in the valley. The stories and yarns spun about these and other notorious characters continue to flow from the pens of every writer so inclined to tell about them.

It could never be said that the old-timers ever tired of telling and retelling the stories of the "Apach'," the gunslinger, the outlaw, and the tough miner. They all had lived right in this valley. In the late 1800s, the discoveries of silver, gold, and copper, and just the plain old fascination of new frontiers to be conquered brought all kinds of characters to this area. The Apache were not too thrilled about all this. This was *their* country, *their* hunting grounds, and thus the stage was set for a confrontation between them and the white men invading their land. The stage was also set for miners in search of wealth and those that came to serve them with the building of towns, stores, livery stables, saloons, and cafes. The outlaw came to prey on those who made their money the legitimate way. The prostitutes came to get in on the act. And then, of course, there were the ranchers, who came to this big country where there was land for the taking to raise their herds and build their empires. This was and is fascinating country.

The romance of the Old West will always be with us. What youngster hasn't played "cowboys and Indians?" You want to draw a crowd? Start talking about the tales surrounding these pioneers.

I was talking to a good friend of mine the other day who has, in the last few years, made many trips to Europe. He says that people there are very taken with the cowboy, the Indian, and the West in general. No, the stories and the legends of this time and this place, especially, will not cease. I'm sure I am repeating many an author's and historian's explanation for all this, but I do know that people everywhere have always admired individuality, the tough but gentle rancher-cowboy, the last-ditch fight of the Indian for his land. It was a period like no other, in a setting like no other. When I lived there, there was no lack of stories, and it was like living in a history book. Old-timers said over and over that when you get "too sissy" to live in Willcox, you moved to Tombstone. Local pride, I guess.

It's too bad that the movie and television writers have gone so far afield in their portrayal of the West and its inhabitants in that era. Had they done their research, they would have found the true tales and stories to be more to their audience's liking than what was put on film. Sure, they have to make the whole thing romantic and daring, but there was plenty of that in the real experiences of these people.

I have to be quick to say, however, that a lot of these so-called "true" happenings became just a bit more glamorous as they were told over and over through the years. The storyteller of my time had grown older, and even though he or she had had firsthand experiences, somehow we just knew that all of what they told could not have happened that way. Yet, I would rather rely on their memories than all of the movie writers combined.

It was my privilege to know many of these men and women who had lived in that era. They were still around, and they loved to sit by the hour and relive their younger days with people I had only heard about or read about in novels and history books.

My dad, too, was completely taken by this country and its history. When I was a boy, we visited the site of Indian massacres and famous gunfights, well-known ranches, ghost towns, old mines, and, best of all, the people themselves. Dad began to collect all the books he could find on the area, be they fact or fiction.

I am going to tell you some of the stories that I heard from these fascinating and wonderful people. My versions of some of these happenings may or may not jibe, right down the line, with some accepted versions, but "let the chips fall where they may." My sources were the people who had been there or who lived perhaps only a few miles away from all the action. There are many inaccuracies, I'm sure, because these tales were not written down but traveled by word of mouth.

The other day I read in the paper an account of the demise of Johnny Ringo (John Ringgold). According to most people, he was one of the most feared gunmen and, supposedly, the fastest man with a gun around. His prowess with a gun is not disputed, but according to many who I talked with, Ringo was just a plain downright thief and "no-good." His only virtue, according to these people, was that he was fast with a gun. Otherwise, he was a most undesirable character.

Back when Tombstone was in its heyday, the town could get pretty "hot" for men like Ringo. Either the law was after them, or they were in trouble with others who they just didn't want to run into in the street. When this was the case, there was always a refuge, Galeyville, a small mining and milling town up in the north part of the Chiricahuas. The mining played out, but the town kept on as an outlaw refuge. To get there, these boys got into the saddle and hightailed it across the valley, up through the town of Sunglow, at the foot of the mountains and at the entrance into Turkey Creek Canyon. Up through the canyon they'd go, over the top at Rustler's Park (a pretty paradise of a high mountain meadow), right on top of the mountains, down the other side, and into Galeyville.

Galeyville was run by one very infamous rounder by the name of Curly Bill Brocius. He was the unofficial leader of the town and an official leader in that he got himself elected to several posts, such as the town council, and once he was elected to an office that might be similar to our present-day county supervisor. Curly Bill earned his living by leading raids into Mexico and areas close to the border to take whatever he could from the Mexican supply and gold and silver trains. Curly Bill and his bunch would hit the train, take the loot, and disappear back into the mountains to Galeyville. There, he and the boys would spend their loot in riotous living until they ran out — then back on another raid.

Anyway, all the undesirables and so-called "scum" from all over the area knew that Galeyville was a haven away from the law where they could reside with good ol' Curly till things quieted down back in Tombstone, Pearce, Bisbee, or wherever.

Well, as I heard it, Ringo was not popular in Tombstone at times, and he was forever and always at odds with the Earps. Ringo may have been fast, and he may have had confidence in what he could do with a gun, but he wasn't about to tangle with Wyatt Earp, nor Virgil, for that matter. In case you don't know, Wyatt and Virgil Earp were part of the law in Tombstone. Their younger brother Morgan also lived there, but I never did hear what his gainful employment was, if any. As I once heard it, Ringo and another unsavory character, "Injun" Charlie, planned the murder of Morgan Earp, with Charlie actually doing the dirty work.

Well, Ringo and Wyatt got "sideways" with one another, and Ringo, being the fearless character he was, took himself out of Tombstone as fast as his horse would take him. Now, here's where my version of what went on differs from a lot of other versions, but this is the way I heard it from an old-time rancher who lived there. Remember the little town of Sunglow that I just told about? Right next to town was a large ranch house, owned by Mr. Sanders. Mr. Sanders ("Hod" to everyone who knew him) was a loner, in fact, down-right anti-social. He wanted nothing to do with other humans unless forced to, and he made this generally known. His ranch was off-limits, period. Sunglow existed as a lumber town. The residents went into Turkey Creek Canyon and brought out the trees to be made into timbers for the mines, in Pearce and Bisbee, especially. One thing they knew: don't cross old Hod, in fact, stay away from him at all costs. They were downright afraid of him, and rightfully so. He was tough and he was mean.

Along came Ringo, as the story goes, and Hod Sanders caught him riding across his ranch. He accosted Ringo and told him to get his "blankety-blank" body off his ranch, telling Ringo that he would let him go this time, but that if he ever found him on his place again, he'd kill him and ask questions later. Exit Mr. Ringo, riding fast. Well, somehow the word got around the little town. How that happened is anybody's guess, but the people were aware of what had happened. Ringo continued on and kept his rendezvous with his old buddy, Curly Bill. He resided in worry-free Galeyville for some months until the lure of the bright lights and all the action took him back to Tombstone. He figured that his problems had disappeared with time, but you have to remember, too, that Ringo hated the Earps and vowed that some way or somehow he'd get 'em.

Events were taking place in Tombstone that were marking the end of the Earps' days there, and there were many people who shared Ringo's dislike for them. About this time, the murder of Morgan Earp took place; at least, this seems to be the sequence of events. This and other circumstances forced Ringo to look to Galeyville and safety again. Off he rode.

A few days later, the town of Sunglow awakened to find a dead man sitting up in the crotch of an old alligator-bark juniper in back of the Sanders' ranch house. There was a hole in his head, his boots were off and lying on the ground, and his six-gun was holstered with one chamber empty (no casing). That was sometimes usual with gunslingers to leave one chamber open. The townspeople quickly convened a coroner's jury and officially declared it suicide. They buried him at the foot of the tree and hung his six-gun on a nail right at the crotch of the tree, and got out of that area but quick. Thus ended the life and career of Johnny Ringo.

There was a lot of speculation elsewhere in the area as to who could have done Ringo in, but the townspeople of Sunglow knew and they weren't talking. Old Hod Sanders went on to lead his lonely life and never said a word. The gun hung on that tree for years, and the handle finally rusted out. The grave was behind a fence on the boundary of Sanders' ranch. For forty or fifty years, no one ever went behind that fence to get that gun, and there was no marker on that grave until just recently. The gun is gone now, so is Hod, and so is Sunglow.

Wyatt Earp was probably the most famous of the old Western lawmen and one of the most controversial. If you got five people together who knew everything about him, you got five different stories about what kind of a man he was and what he was capable of doing. In talking to the old-timers down in Tombstone, I found that many were pro-Earp and many were anti-Earp. This just about sums up his tenure there in Tombstone.

Most devotees of Western lore are not aware of the many forces at work in Tombstone nor the real role of the old Western sheriff or marshal. To most, Earp was a fast gun and a fearless defender of the law; to put it broadly, a "good guy" rather than a "bad guy." The typical Western movie or television show has been very much responsible for that impression of the man. I guess that all of us want to idealize the whole thing and believe that "black is black and white is white." But it just was not that way with Wyatt and his brothers.

I talked to many a person who had known Wyatt in their younger days or who had listened to their parents expound on his character. Depending on who I visited with, I found strong opinions on both sides of the fence. Only once did I ever hear from someone the real true picture of the times, the conditions and circumstances that made Wyatt what he really was.

I'm sure that most people who ever followed the career of Wyatt Earp know that he had brought law and order to Dodge City, Kansas, and then he and his brothers and Doc Holiday decided on greener pastures and migrated to Tombstone. Wyatt's reputation preceded him, and the town, in need of a marshal, chose him soon after he arrived to do in Tombstone what he had done in Dodge City. Mrs. Macias (pronounced "Mac-ee") knew the Earps and Holliday and all the rest as a young girl. She was the owner of the Rose Tree Inn in Tombstone when I talked to her. That's the site of the largest rose bush or tree in the world, and it's a real tourist attraction. I sat under this beautiful plant with her and talked for hours about the old days. I remember that I had my young son, Mark, with me, and on the desk in her living room was an old picture of Earp. He was tall and thin, with a droopy moustache and sharp features, *one gun* strapped to his side. Mark looked at the picture and, when informed that this was *the* Wyatt Earp, he refused to believe it. At that particular time, Hugh O'Brian, clean-shaven, very handsome, and with *two guns* was holding forth on television as Wyatt — so Mark was not convinced.

Mrs. Macias summed up the situation better than I had ever heard; she clarified many things for me. She said that people did not remember or know that you got the meanest, toughest, hardest character you could find to enforce the law. You also faced facts and accepted the saloons, the gambling, the girls, and all the various vices to be found in a wild boom town such as Tombstone. It was just a part of the deal that the local law got in on the proceeds; they got their cut. It was felt that this arrangement would serve to keep these illegal activities under control, since it was to the benefit of the local lawman's pocket-book to keep it that way. And so it was with Earp. He had his fingers in every-thing. Many people objected, for one reason or another, but not usually on moral grounds. Most of these people were jealous of the things that Wyatt was accumulating and the favors he got. They felt that he could take unfair advan-tage because he was the law. They were right, because he could and did get just about what he wanted from the saloon keepers, the gamblers, and from "Big Nose" Kate, who ran the local bawdy-house.

As Mrs. Macias at the Rose Tree Inn explained further, the sheriff — yes, there was one — was a man named Behan. He was in this official position most of the time Earp was there. Behan didn't like Earp for several reasons, one being that he wasn't getting the "goodies" that Earp and his brothers were. Behan was also in "hand and glove" with the cattlemen around the area who, for various reasons, were just natural-born enemies of the townspeople. It seems they felt that they got "ripped off" by the locals in just about everything, and they felt that Wyatt enjoyed seeing them get taken when they came to town.

Earp was not out for any popularity contests; he ran things with an iron hand. Many people got to hating him and his family and Doc, who had thrown in with them back in Kansas. They objected to Wyatt's "high-handed" ways.

So there it was. Earp, the tough lawman, with his family and his cronies around him, keeping the town under his thumb, agitating the cowboys and ranchers who he kept from "blowing the lid off" when they came to town, and getting well-heeled in the process. The townspeople didn't like this at all. They were jealous of him. And the crooks and thieves feared him.

It has to be said that not all the ranchers were "anti-Earp," because they weren't. Colonel Hooker up at the Sierra Bonita Ranch was his buddy, as were several others, but it seemed that the further away from Tombstone people were, the better they got on with Earp.

So you see, the whole situation wasn't one of black and white. There were many forces at work for and against Wyatt Earp. And he was not one to go around explaining his actions. He did what he thought he ought to at the time, and everyone could "lump" it. And that didn't especially endear him to every-one. With all this, Earp developed enemies. And when the town needed a con-stable or assistant marshal, Wyatt made sure that his brother Virgil got the job, another thorn in many a side.

I could go on with all the tales that have been told about the exploits of Wyatt with his gun, a big long-barreled Buntline, but these have been distorted and played up all out of proportion. Earp was fast, but he didn't meet many out in the street at the drop of a hat as the romantics have the classic Western hero doing. No sir, Earp's job was one of law enforcement, and if someone took it upon themselves to challenge him, Earp was so quick that he would have that Buntline out and bring the barrel down on the challenger's head in such a manner as to render him unconscious. Then he would haul him off to the pokey. Sure, Earp killed some in his time, but not the number he was credited with.

Earp was fearlessly tough, which certainly showed in the big confrontation at the O. K. Corral. When the chips were down, he did whatever seemed necessary — in his own mind. The gunfight probably never needed to have happened, but events had taken place that predicted that the Clantons and their friends and the Earps would have to have a showdown. Many an old-timer down there loves to talk about this classic battle, and most agree on what happened, but there is great disagreement on the necessity for it. Yet it did happen, and although Earp's forces won, the gunfight signaled the end of Wyatt's reign, and he knew it. There were a few bits of unfinished business that had to be taken care of, but Wyatt knew that he was through in Tombstone. This fight, I feel, took something out of Earp. Soon afterward, he, Virgil, and Doc left. Wyatt ended up in Colton, California, living a very quiet and almost sedentary life until he died, a far cry from his life in Dodge City and Tombstone.

Wyatt left his mark, and not only on those infamous cities where he held forth with a badge. He became to his generation and those after him the epitome of the Old West, a legend going on and on with achievements no man could have ever lived up to — nevertheless, he was the "King of the Western Heroes."

Doctor Holliday, that was his name. One of the most interesting of the West's notorious men, he very probably has had more inaccuracies printed and told about him than any other Western character. Most movies and television shows have the good Doctor as a doctor — an M.D., or some such. But he wasn't — he was a dentist.

Doc was raised in a well-to-do Southern family and raised a gentleman. Everyone who knew him told about his soft Southern accent and his very perfect manners. Knowing this about the man, it was quite a paradox that he was also one of the meanest and roughest men around in those days. The hallmark of his personality was his "don't give a damn" attitude. This was understandable, because Doc was a bitter man. He felt that life had dealt him a bitter blow, and he took out his bitterness on everyone around him.

He had been raised in the "good life," had gone on to become a dentist. The blow struck quickly after that, when he found he had consumption (tuberculosis), and the doctors told him he would soon die. They urged him to go west.

They certainly did not predict a cure but thought he might live a little longer if he did go to a drier climate. Actors who have portrayed Doc wander around coughing, with a handkerchief to their faces all the time. Well, that isn't too far wrong. He did suffer from an advanced stage of tuberculosis, and he felt lousy all of the time.

He had been told that he would die soon, and that, coupled with feeling sick all the time, twisted his personality to the point that he just did not care what happened to himself. At the same time, he became judgmental and took it on himself to deal with people any way he wanted to; he was always right and they were wrong. He was ready to back up this conviction with a gun or fists or anything else. If he got killed in the course of events, "what the hell" — he was going to die anyway.

A good example of his attitude was a story told to me by an elderly lady who had lived in Tombstone at the time. She rode her buggy into town after a few days of continuous rain. The streets were a sea of mud. She maneuvered her buggy close to the wooden sidewalk, which was about two feet higher than the street. With great difficulty, she finally got as close as she could. She jumped for the walk and made it, except for a part of her long dress, which dragged along in the mud. Standing right there in front of her was a town loafer, who just stood and watched the whole proceeding, never offering a hand. Up strode Holliday, after he had watched the whole thing, and whipped out his little derringer, calmly shooting the ill-mannered loafer in the leg. The loafer went down with a yell of pain. Holliday stood over him and said, "You blankety-blank so-and-so. You always help a lady out of her buggy — next time I'll kill you." He turned and inquired as to the lady's well-being and then strode off.

Not much is known about Holliday's first travels in the West until he showed up in Dodge City as a gambler, a profession that he made his life's work. It was there, in Dodge, that he took up with the Earps. It was a very strange friendship. They all liked each other and took to each other quickly, but there never seemed to be the closeness that you find among friends, and there never was a lot of conversation between these men. They just seemed to understand each other, and when they needed one another, they were together. When the Earps pulled out of Dodge, of course Holliday was with them.

He set up shop in the Oriental Saloon, most of the time, but was known to also hold forth at the gaming tables at the Crystal Palace and others. His alliance with the Earps was well-known, and this combination kept the local citizenry in line. As feared as Wyatt was, everyone was literally petrified of Holliday. They knew he didn't care what happened to himself and that he would do just about anything to achieve his own ends. You just gotta be pretty scared of someone like that.

He seemed to live a fairly peaceful life in Tombstone, although there are some tales floating around of his wounding or killing someone over some trivial matter, usually arising out of a card game. How true these are, is anyone's guess.

Television and movie writers always portrayed Doc wandering around with six-guns strapped to his side. No one who knew him agrees with this. According to my sources, he never once carried a six-gun. He always carried two derringers in his vest pockets, one on each side. The times that he went actually "gunning" for someone, and the O. K. Corral gunfight was one of them, he wore a long frock coat, and down on his right side, hung from a leather thong on his belt, he carried a sawed-off ten-gauge shotgun. He would flip his coat back, grab the gun, and let go as quickly as any "gunnie" with a six-gun. And with much more devastating results. Knowing this man's personality and his bitterness toward life in general, it just seemed to fit that he would carry such a weapon. They say that, at the O. K. Corral, his first blast with this cannon tore Tom McLauery in half and took the underside of a horse away. Then, as was his style, he would pull out his two "little jobs" and fire away with them. Yes sir, he was a very sadistic man.

Many particular incidents about this man are not known. He traded his dentist's tools for the cards and dice of a gambler, and as far as anyone knew, he never even mentioned his dental training.

The last episode of the good "Doctor" took place when he, Virgil, and Wyatt rode out of Tombstone for the last time, on their way to Tucson to catch a train for California. Morgan Earp had been recently murdered by "Injun Charlie" with Ringo's planning, and the O. K. Corral shootout and some other events had occurred that pointed the way for these three to depart. I don't feel for one minute that Doc felt it necessary to leave, but without his friends, the Earps, it was his time, too.

The train was in the station that summer night and would not pull out for the west until early the next morning. It so happened that these three knew that "Injun" Charlie had taken refuge in Tucson. They boarded the train, and as it began to get dark, Doc left the train, not returning until after midnight. Then he got back on the train and said to Wyatt and Virgil, "It's taken care of." To this, the pair replied, "Thanks, Doc." They shook hands all around, said their goodbyes, and Doc left the train. The next morning, officials in Tucson found the body of "Injun" Charlie.

It was a strange friendship these men felt for one another. They didn't seem to socialize with one another; in fact, just the opposite. Upon seeing one another on the street, they would nod briefly, then be on their way. I'm sure that they got together at times when few were aware of it. Yet the general public knew that there was a bond between them, especially Wyatt and Doc. What happened in Tucson was typical of their actions.

What is very strange, however, is that these men never did contact each other after that last night in Tucson, as far as I ever heard. Doc, who had originally come to the West to die at an early age, appeared next in Leadville, Colorado, plying his trade. I heard from some that he got into some scrapes up there, but nothing of much consequence. Later, as an older man, he lived in Glenwood Springs, Colorado, and he died there, having lived many, many years on borrowed time.

I have mentioned Curly Bill Brocius, the "all-everything" of Galeyville. By that I mean that he controlled the town and turned it into a refuge for all manner of folks who just did not want to have much to do with the law. From what I gather, Curly seemed to just appear on the scene — he didn't seem to have any origin. He was known to have frequented all of the towns in the area but not to have lived in any one for very long. He wore out his welcome pretty quick, so he soon found that remote Galeyville was the place for him. Here he could be long far away from the law, and he could conduct his sorties into Mexico and then disappear back into the mountains. It was a perfect deal. And no lawman or posse in their right mind was about to try to storm this outlaw bastion.

Curly held forth and decided to become a local politician along with his other activities. There's a story about one election held in Galeyville in which Curly emerged an overwhelming victor. It was for an office you might compare to today's county supervisor. When the results were in, the votes in favor of Bill exceeded all of the known populace for miles around. It appeared that the local graveyards' inhabitants voted, and that all animals such as goats, burros, chickens, and horses also voted under all kinds of assumed names. The territorial government was going to go to Galeyville and conduct an investigation but got to thinking better of it and didn't go. One official was heard to remark, "Well, I guess we just don't have accurate figures on the population and there are more people than we thought." They weren't about to challenge the "Boss" in his own bailiwick.

Not much is known about the enmity of Wyatt Earp for Curly, but it is well known that Wyatt had no use for the latter. It stuck in Wyatt's craw that this character could live a pretty free and easy existence. In addition, most of Curly's looting and robbery was conducted against Mexicans and in Mexico, especially during the years that Wyatt was the law in Tombstone — and Wyatt really had no jurisdiction. Nevertheless, Wyatt wanted Curly, and he wanted him badly.

According to the well-known story, Wyatt, in one of his last gestures before leaving, decided to travel to the Sierra Bonita Ranch north of Willcox to pay a visit to his old friend, Colonel Hooker. He set out, but a few days later he returned to Tombstone with the story that he had ridden into Sulphur Springs for water and there ran into Curly Bill. A gunfight ensued, and Wyatt claimed he killed Curly and left his body. A posse of sorts was gathered immediately to ride out to Sulphur Springs and bring in the body. But they found nothing.

Wyatt stuck steadfastly to his story that he had indeed done in the outlaw, but there were many doubters. The only sure thing is that Curly Bill was never seen again in those parts. The story does have an ending. Years later, a number of people made trips to Mexico and returned with a tale of having seen Curly, alive and well, married to a Mexican lady and living in a big *hacienda* way down in the interior of Mexico. This story persisted among the old-timers of my day, and one old cowboy I knew claimed to have actually visited with Curly. Well, no one ever knew for sure, but whatever happened at Sulphur Springs marked the end of Curly's presence in the valley.

I could go on and on about all types of characters who roamed this area but were not so well known, and many who led the good life and were there to make something of the valley and the towns in which they lived, but we would never end. The one thing I did hope to accomplish was to tell a little about the men themselves and some of the more revealing stories about them. One needs to write a whole book on the interesting people of this era.

I could tell you of Colonel Hooker and his famous ranch and over one hundred cowboys on his payroll out at the Sierra Bonita. He certainly didn't need that many to run his ranch. He just had his own army. Those were Indian days, and a lot of unsavory characters were around, so maybe he thought he needed this kind of protection. I heard from many that the good Colonel had ideas of creating his own empire up there in the north of the valley, but for some reason he never realized this ambition.

Billy the Kid, usually thought of as a New Mexican, lived for a time in the Bonita area, and he killed his first victim in back of the Bonita store.

Then there is James Tevis, who came to the area as a young man to work with the old Butterfield Stage Line and other endeavors, and who actually engaged in physical battle with Cochise himself. His writings of the exploits of the Army and the Indians are the best. Present-day Bowie was originally called Tevis-town after this gentleman.

Speaking of those who were the builders, I would be remiss if I did not tell about the young man, E. Melvin Jones, who was born in Russellville and got his schooling across the Graham Mountains at Fort Thomas. This boy was the son of one Captain Jones, who made his living as a cavalryman. His job was, with his platoon, to convoy the big freight wagons on a circuit from Sunglow to Pearce, to Russellville and Ft. Grant, and on around the mountain to Fort Thomas. Until the boy was either seven or nine years of age, I am not sure, the family lived in this little hamlet in the Dragoons. But there was no school, so the parents decided that the family would have to move to a town with a school. They chose Fort Thomas, an Army post that boasted a fine school. Here the young man grew up. This young man had a vision, and he made that vision come true. E. Melvin Jones went on to found Lions International, one of the largest civic clubs in the world, devoted to helping the blind and involved in all types of civic work.

Most everyone knew of Wyatt, Virgil, and Morgan Earp, but few ever knew that there was another brother, Warren. Warren frequented Willcox most of the time, and not much is ever heard of his activities in Tombstone. He also was a bully, and he enjoyed picking on someone, especially if they were smaller or just plain scared of the Earp name. He would go into a saloon and get himself "loaded," then proceed to "unload" on any close victim that filled the bill. One such character was a fellow named Boyett, a small man and not one of the town's more upstanding citizens. He became a favorite whipping boy of Warren, who abused him physically as well as verbally. Finally one night, Boyett had had enough. He took off out of the saloon after one of these sessions with Warren, vowing that he was going to get a gun and come back and kill him. Warren, figuring him for a coward, egged him on. "Do it, you skinny little S. O. B.," Warren yelled after him.

Some fifteen minutes later, Boyett came through the doors, yelling and cursing at Warren, and proceeded to fire two shots. That didn't stop Warren, who kept on advancing on Boyett. Three more shots were fired, and Warren was killed. After a hearing, Warren Earp was buried in the old cemetery in Willcox. To this day, I have not talked to anyone who ever heard that Boyett suffered any consequences for his deed.

The old grave marker is gone and has been for many years. Some say that a number of years after Warren Earp's demise, enterprising characters who were making old Boothill cemetery in Tombstone into a tourist attraction came and, under cover of darkness, stole the grave marker to take it back to stand in Tombstone. But Warren Earp isn't buried there — he's in the old Willcox Boothill cemetery.

Tall Men — Tall Tales

The stories, the tales, the yarns flowed thick and fast around many a camp-fire, in the front room of a ranch house, on the street corners, and other places, but the pioneers I knew never tired of telling about this character or that, about this incident or that. We should have had tape recorders to get all of this down. Because now it's too late and these people are gone. A lot of this has been put into print over the years, so much has been preserved. As I travel the valley today, I can't help but think of these people that lived here and of the history they made.

The Town Conscience

HIS NAME was Jess Moore. He was the law in Willcox and in just about all of northern Cochise County. That's not the way it was supposed to be, but that's the way it was. The sheriff of the county knew that if there was a problem or situation that needed taking care of, why, Jess would take care of it. Sure, we had a deputy in town, too, but when it came to law and order in that area, everyone looked to Jess. Nearly all of my life in Willcox, that's the way it was.

Jess was a big man, with piercing eyes that looked right through you and seemed to see in every direction. He never missed a thing, which was a prerequisite to staying healthy in his profession in that time and place. He was the last of an era. He was the rough, tough lawman, the judge and jury in many an instance, and, in his way, a kindly and considerate fatherly type, although this quality didn't come through too often. Everyone in the Willcox area had respect for and were somewhat fearful of Jess. Many an unruly and disobedient child straightened right up and behaved for his or her parents when threatened with being taken before Jess Moore.

Jess felt that Willcox was "his town," and so, by golly, he was going to run it his way — which he did. I certainly don't remember the town citizenry giving Jess a bad time. No sir!

He carried a long and heavily weighted nightstick. When the occasion arose he could wield that stick very effectively. I don't suppose that Jess was afraid of anything or anyone. He recognized the need for the boys to let off steam once in a while, and he felt that a good healthy fistfight now and then at a dance or outside a saloon was all right, just so long as things didn't get out of hand. When they did, he waded in with that big stick of his and rendered many of those boys into unconscious states. They then spent the night or a few nights in the local calaboose, which by all standards was pretty bad. It was an old stuccoed adobe building with bare walls and not much room. So the boys had their good times but were careful not to arouse Jess to action.

Jess took great pride in his ability, taking it upon himself to look after young and old alike. I'm just not sure that he ever held the official job of truant

56

officer, but he sure performed those duties as well. Many a boy and girl returned to school willingly after being rounded up by Jess.

Car ownership among the high school set was very rare in those days, but one young man in school did own a car. When I say "car," I say it cautiously, because this vehicle ran like a car, had four wheels and other necessary items, but it sure didn't look like a car. It was a "strip-down" if I ever saw one. The proud owner was Red Fanning. Red was somewhat of a rowdy, the local dragster. He turned corners on two wheels and brought fear to any motorist or pedestrian in his vicinity. Well, Jess finally decided that enough was enough. He caught up with Red one day and confiscated the keys to the car, telling Red that he was now afoot and would remain so until he, Jess, decided differently. That vehicle sat parked on the street for several weeks until Jess thought Red had learned his lesson. Can you visualize that action today? Might solve some problems.

We had a CCC camp out in Pinery Canyon in the Chiricahuas. For the younger set, this was the Civilian Conservation Corps, which provided jobs for unemployed young men. Men lived in these camps much as in an Army camp, and they were involved in all kinds of projects to improve our national parks and forests. When these young men came to town after a week or two of hard work, they were another group that Jess had to contend with. By early Saturday night they were usually feeling no pain, and many of them got caught up with the idea of creating destruction and mayhem. When this occurred, Jess came around wielding his nightstick, and the culprits took up residence in his jail. The commanding officer of the CCC objected to this manhandling of his men, but to no avail, so a number of the men decided that they would gang up on Jess their next time in town and teach him a lesson. Sure enough, one night down on Railroad Avenue, about fifteen of these stalwarts waylayed Jess. A wild and bloody melee ensued, and when the dust cleared, thirteen prostrate bodies littered the sidewalk until they were carted off to the jailhouse. From that time on, no more trouble came out of the CCC boys.

Another local character was Joe Clark. Joe was an old reprobate whose means of support was a well-hidden mystery; he was up in years but seemed to survive in some form or another. Evidently his life as a drifter, con-artist, performer of sorts, and all-around ne'er-do-well had been his way for many years. I can remember him well, very tan, wandering around town without a shirt, with blue eyes and a shaggy mane of white hair. He was known to make his home in Willcox and, sometimes, in Douglas. In Willcox he resided in an old shack across the tracks. Now, Joe liked the girls, even in his advanced stage of life. In those days, one could go to Mexico, going through the proper channels, and bring Mexican women into this country to work as domestic help. As you might guess, some men brought up women for that purpose, ostensibly, but actually they were interested in these women performing other duties. And so it was with good old Joe.

One night Jess Moore came into the Rix Saloon and advised a ranch foreman, Bert Gardner, that he had wind of the fact that Joe had a young Mexican girl with him over at his shack and that he was going over to arrest him. Jess wanted Bert to accompany him. Bert asked why he had to come along and objected to being involved, but Jess insisted. As Bert said later, "You don't argue with Jess," and along he went. Upon arriving at the shack, Jess, not worried about any formalities, proceeded to break through the door. There was Joe, in bed with the Mexican girl. Jess roared, "What the hell are you doing with this girl, Joe?" Joe pointed to an open Bible on the nightstand and stated that he was only giving this girl a Bible lesson. Jess didn't believe this and told Joe to get his clothes on, that he was going to jail. When Joe was fully dressed, Jess told Bert to take Joe to the pokey. Bert replied, "Why me? What are you going to do?" Jess replied, "Bert, just do what I say. I'm staying right here to continue the lesson."

I've already related some of my experiences in playing for dances, and I've told of the wild and woolly occasion up at Dos Cabezas. That dance was completely out of hand from the time it started, and Jess and the deputy, Dee Tucker, made trip after trip to Willcox to take the wrongdoers to jail. Well, at first it didn't occur to us that there were more going to jail than that place could hold. Then we finally saw with our own eyes that Jess had solved the problem in his own manner.

The old dirt road back to Willcox wound down and out of Dos Cabezas proper and then more or less straightened out on the flats. The telephone lines ran right along the road on both sides of it. In our haste to get out of that place, we didn't notice until we were down the road a few miles and the day was lightening what Jess had done with all the excess miscreants at that dance. Yes sir, when the jail got full, why, Jess had just tied these boys to the telephone posts, and there they were, one at each pole all the way to town.

When Jess left his post as the town marshal, law enforcement in Willcox was never the same again. With him died an era. He was a good man in many ways and a scoundrel in others, but we in Willcox always felt very secure knowing that Jess Moore was out there somewhere protecting us. He will never be forgotten.

Red and Black – Fight! Fight!

HIGH SCHOOL DAYS are usually looked back on as the fun time of your life. Anyway, they sure were for me. Sure, I had a ball in college, too, but there isn't anything to equal high school days, especially when you live in a small town where everything revolves around high school activities. Many years later, I said that it's a good thing there are such activities in these small towns, or the social life would be "zilch."

The old school building itself is gone now, but I can still see it sitting there in the middle of town with the twin domes gleaming silver in the sunlight. Our school faced east, with the two domes above the entrance to the building and a large balcony above that. Off to the right, as you came in, were the offices. There were a number of doors, and you entered a large foyer with the trophy case straight ahead of you against the wall. The hallway stretched away from this area to the north and the south with classrooms on both sides. Directly in back of the wall where the trophies were was the auditorium, on a little higher level, and the basement level, where shop was held ("manual arts" was the correct name then). We had a split-level school. You went down the hall on either side and went upstairs one floor and into the auditorium, or you could keep on going another flight of stairs and you would come to the third story, between the domes. This was the home economics room, which doubled at times as a cafeteria, although that was short-lived, as I remember. Going down one level of stairs you could also go out to the back of the building where the gymnasium stood. This old relic stood almost directly in back of the main building. The main gym was in the middle of this monstrosity, with the boys' locker room and showers on the left and the girls' on the right. Tennis courts flanked the main building. The Vocational Agriculture building, much smaller than the others, was directly in back of the north tennis courts. Clear out in back of this entire complex was the football field.

I wanted to give some idea of the school's layout so you might understand where everything was as we go along. It was functional but outmoded. We all understood that it had been condemned for years — or at least that was the story.

Back in those days, it was a real achievement to arrive at the age of high school. We had a little extra bonus because we attended eighth grade in the high school building. When we reached this magical age, we were really "hot stuff" because we were up with the big kids. We lorded it over the rest of the grade school kids, making sure that we didn't let on how we in turn were victims of the superiority complex of the high school kids. They looked down on us as strictly pests and had no time for us immature "invaders." We were tolerated — just barely.

It was a big occasion to reach this status, but since we were fish out of water, we eighth graders accomplished very little except to graduate from grade school and bask in the glories of high school. Our teachers were, for the most part, the high school teachers. (I often wondered about that, years later when I was on a school board. It must have created problems, but if it did, we kids were not aware of it.) The high school principal was also stuck with us. Our principal was Mr. Tom Sawyer — there's a name for you. He was a slightly-built man, losing his hair, very dignified, and he wore a very formal suit at all times. At least, that's the way I remember him. He ran the school with an iron hand but was a fair man. I was always impressed with him, and we all respected him. He had two sons, Bill and Ed, who were just about my age, and we were good friends. I went to their house often but always with the awareness that I was in the principal's house. Mr. Sawyer later got out of education, becoming very involved with the American Legion. He took a job working full-time with the Legion, and we heard that the family had moved to the East. Later, Mr. Sawyer was the founding father of the Freedom Foundation of Valley Forge and became its first director. He held this post for many years before retiring. And years later I re-established my old friendships with Bill and Ed when they came back to the state to make their home. Needless to say, Mr. Tom Sawyer, my first principal, had a profound effect on me.

When I finally became a freshman, I was really on my way. But, there again, the old seniority system prevailed and we frosh were low men on the totem pole. We were forced to wear our "beanies," and we went through "initiation" for several weeks at the beginning of school. We were forced to do all kinds of menial tasks and in general were fearful each day of the terrible things that might happen, although they didn't. So we eventually settled down to become full-fledged members of the high school.

I just have to get in a little philosophical reminiscing and a little bit of sermonizing to the young people of today. We older people feel that we were really in the know in those days, and as we have gotten older, we feel that we have an insight into a lot of situations that the young people today do not

Willcox Union High School (COURTESY "ARIZONA RANGE NEWS," WILLCOX)

have. As I look back on my high school days and I see the young people today — and don't forget, I have raised five children — I don't see the kids today having the genuine, clean-cut fun we did. I don't see the loyalty and the truly sincere respect for elders that we had then. There was a feeling of something like awe for most of our teachers. If we were involved in athletics, the coach was the all-seeing, all-powerful, and all-knowledgeable leader, and we were not about to cross him in any way. Don't get me wrong, we had some teachers we just couldn't stand and we bedeviled them in almost any way we could, and we weren't always the good little kids I make us sound like. But for the most part we were happy to be there. Almost without exception, we wanted to get what we could out of our time in high school. We enjoyed it. We liked our teachers, maybe because we were brought up with the idea that you did what they told you and there just weren't too many areas of conflict. And nearly all of us had some kind of true ambition to accomplish something, either through further education or in some other area.

I know that there is a lot more freedom for the student today. He or she is more free to question. There are many more courses offered, and there are programs that we would have been astounded to see. The coaching is far superior to what it was in my day. Young athletes today receive all the latest methods and training and coaching skills available, so they are better athletes than we were, in that respect.

But to me the proof of the pudding is in the eating. I think of the people who I grew up with and attended school with, and their achievements have been outstanding. In a small school like that, we all mingled and participated, something on the order of a large family. My class and the classes before and after our group turned out many, many men and women who have made their mark in this world — and made it big! Many have achieved success in the field of education; one is vice-president of a college. One is the head of the science department of a large university and has been associated with the Atomic Energy Commission in several capacities. One is a well-known state highway engineer, another is the head of personnel and employment for the largest natural gas company in the world. Another has become a very wealthy real estate investor, rancher, and oil man. Another just retired as a colonel in the Strategic Air Command, only because of medical reasons. I've mentioned that one of my good friends who took music lessons from my mother appeared on Broadway in a number of musicals, went touring with groups all over the country, and still continues his career in television and music. I didn't mention names, but I will mention that of Rex Allen, who went on to become a well-known Western movie and television star and now does a lot of personal appearances and narrating for the Walt Disney features. I could go on and talk about so many that have come to levels of success in all types of endeavor that surely surprised many of the townspeople, and even the people themselves. It has been remarkable what has happened over the years, and the residents of Willcox are still amazed and proud of the products of this small school.

I'm sure that this kind of accomplishment has to be some sort of exception. It just isn't in the cards to have a group of young people from one small town, or even a large one, come forth and make their mark as these have. But I wanted to tell you about these people to illustrate what I was saying. You cannot argue with success, so our schools in Willcox and our parents and the town leaders certainly must have done something right.

I can remember getting on the train to return to Willcox for the first time after World War II was over. I was still in the Navy, but I was going home to spend Christmas of 1945 — my first holidays spent at home for some four years. I had my bars and stars on my uniform, indicating that I had been a lot of places and had engaged in a lot of activity in the Navy, when the conductor came to get my ticket. Just as he reached my seat and took a look at me he said, "Bet you're going to Willcox." I assented. He continued, "I knew it. Every time I see one of you boys with all that "salad" on your chest on this train, I know he's headed for Willcox. All you boys really have a record in the service — I never saw anything like it." That filled me with pride, and it was certainly true. When the call came to go to war, the boys from Willcox answered and did their job well.

So you can see why I get impatient with a lot of the school deficiencies and problems today. Of course, I do have to be fair and honest and put practically the entire blame on the parents. They have not performed very well when it comes to raising children today, and they have attempted to let the schools do the job for them and also take the blame. Many will disagree with me, but I do have some proof that the old tried-and-true methods of basic teaching, discipline, parental concern, and concern from the townspeople can do the trick. I certainly agree with going forward with new technology in teaching, but that has become the ruling factor and not a supplemental one. We have too many educators engrossed in pushing their own careers and tied up with all kinds of idiotic programs that keep the classroom teacher from teaching the kids. They're too busy being bookkeepers and statisticians to do a job of teaching. I could go on but this isn't the purpose of the book — I got on a crusade.

In a small school like ours, everyone did everything. It had to be that way, or nothing got done. I got involved in activities that I know I would not have anywhere else, had I been in a larger school. We wanted to do these things and to achieve because the whole town became involved and interested in whatever went on at the school. My junior and senior year I participated in the class play. We not only acted, but we got out and put out the placards in the store windows advertising the play and we sold tickets — and we played to a packed house. I've always been accused of being a pretty good "ham," so I enjoyed the whole thing immensely. I can still see us up there on that stage, holding forth.

I believe it was in my junior year that we had a very vivacious and pretty teacher come into our midst as the business and commerce teacher, which meant everything from typing to economics, and so on. Her name was Hazel Ahlgren, later Huffman. All the boys got a pretty good crush on her. She was small with blonde hair and blue eyes, and we all developed a great interest in every course she taught. In my senior year she asked me to be the editor of the annual, "The

Roundup." I was flattered but apprehensive, because I was not that confident about my abilities along this line. But I took it on, mainly because she had asked me to do it, and somehow we got it done. I'll long remember that whole episode, because I soon had another female enter my life at this point. That year, one of the prettiest girls I had ever seen entered school — she had dark hair, dark eyes, and all the features in the right place, and she wanted to be part of the editorial staff of the annual. I was all for it, and so was Miss Ahlgren. Jean Divelbess was her name; I wonder what ever happened to her. All the boys went ape. They were all in love with her, I'm sure. She knew it and played it to the hilt — she really knew how. I can remember years later finally realizing what a flirt she was. At the time, though, we were all smitten, and I had the enviable duty of working with her on our project. So, many hours of intensive work went into the production of that book, whether we needed to or not. The result of all this was that I scored the biggest *coup* of my school career: she went to the junior-senior prom with me. That was a real occasion. I wore a white jacket tux with all the trimmings, got Jean a nice corsage, and Dad let me have the family car for the occasion. It was an event to remember. After graduation she moved from Willcox, and I've not heard of her since. She had been the love of my life for a few short months, and she disappeared from it almost as soon as she entered it. Ah, well, such is life!

I've told you about my playing the trumpet in the dance band. Boy, we were big stuff in that little band. But I also sang in the Glee Club and a boys' quartet, and I was in the band and brass quartet. I even played solos for a number of events, even for church.

The first band teacher we had when I entered school was Jim Williams, a large man, on the fat side. He had been a piano player in a dance band for years, on one of the cruise ships running from our West Coast to China and the Orient. But Jim's wife got pretty tired of that life, so "Big Jim" (as we kids called him) went back to school for a summer, got his teaching certificate, and we ended up with him. You had to like the guy: he was more like a big brother than a teacher. I guess that's why I still call him Jim rather than Mr. Williams. He was a good musician, and could he ever play the piano! But his heart wasn't in teaching high school kids the finer points of music.

We had about thirty-five members of the band, then, and we were pretty terrible, and he knew it. In order to create some real "pizazz" and to take the listeners' minds off the music, he outfitted us in cowboy outfits — bright red satin shirts, black Western pants, black cowboy boots, and black hats. Can you believe that get-up? Well, we thought it pretty "jazzy," and we stuck with it all the time I was in school.

64

Big Jim would have preferred the dance band business, but he stayed in teaching for two years, and he taught us some things. I will never forget band rehearsals. They were right after lunch, a terrible time to have it. Big Jim would get up there, pounding his baton on the stand and bellowing at us (he had a voice you could hear all over the school). When we made a big "clinker" and he had run out of patience, he'd yell, "You kids couldn't play 'Come to Jesus' in the key of C." Instead of achieving the right response from us, it always resulted in a lot of snickers and smirks. Then he would really get mad and usually broke the baton over the stand. We achieved some measure of success in the band contests at the fairs, but we certainly were not polished musicians.

I liked Jim Williams, but many of the parents didn't. After two years, he left us, with a sigh of relief — and probably under distressing circumstances. When he left, he had a beautiful radio-phonograph that also had short-wave channels on it. He wanted me to keep it for him because he really did not know what or where he would be. He told me to keep it and he would return for it when he was settled. But he never came back for it, and I never heard from him again. That radio became a real treasure of mine. I can remember staying up very late at night, when I was supposed to have gone to bed, with the music on low so the rest of the family could not hear. I listened to ships at sea and to calls from all over the world. But the best thing was to listen to all the different dance bands, late at night, playing from the famous, beautiful ballrooms all over the country. I listened to the bands from the Trianon in Los Angeles, the Meadowbrook in New Jersey, the Trocadero in Los Angeles, the fabulous Coconut Grove, you name it. All the bands fascinated me. I got so I could tell the band just by listening to their style and arrangements. I heard them all: Miller, Basie, Glen Gray, Johnny Long, Joe Venuti, Ted Fiorito, Woody Herman, Duke Ellington, Will Bradley. You name 'em, I knew 'em. It became a real hobby for me, one that I still enjoy today. That was real music! Many years later, as I traveled extensively, I found these great swing and jazz musicians wherever they were appearing and I saw them in person. And I will never forget Big Jim Williams. Whether or not he was able to teach me much in the way of performing, he certainly left me, through his own love of that type of music and the gift of the radio, with an appreciation and enjoyment for that music that gets stronger through the years.

My music director for the last two years of high school was a completely different type of person, Mr. Delight (Dee) Maynard. He was tall, thin, sandy-haired, and had, would you believe, a nice little well-trimmed moustache. In those days that little moustache was not a thing of beauty and a joy to behold as they are now. In fact, we all were inclined to feel that our new music teacher was a little on the "sissy" side. But it didn't take long to find out differently. He was all business, and there was a real air of magnetism about the man. Before we knew it, we were a band of almost sixty people. He could get young people interested, and he had all of us playing music that we had only heard of. We soon found ourselves realizing that we were pretty good and that we might go somewhere with our music. We presented a lot of concerts that we had never done before, and we even became a legitimate marching band — still in those cowboy outfits, however. (Try marching in cowboy boots sometime and you'll see what I mean.)

Every year, the area music contests were held at Gila Junior College (now known as Eastern Arizona Junior) in Thatcher. All the bands, smaller groups, and soloists descended on this small campus from high schools throughout east central Arizona. There, for several days, the brass ensembles, various soloists, and bands would perform, judged by experts. We did not compete directly with one another, but we competed for ratings. The best rating you could receive was that of "Superior," then "Excellent," then "Good," and then "Go Back and Start Over," or some such. Our band, brass quartet, boys' quartet, and my trumpet solo were all rated "Superior." This was in my junior year, and our new director was so happy with these results that he decided to have some of us enter the national regional contests to be held in Fresno, California.

At this same time, Dee's brother was the director of music for Globe High School, and he had a number of students he wanted to enter in this same contest. These two put their heads together and it was arranged that five of us from Willcox and five from Globe would meet in Globe and go on to Fresno together. There was a small problem of money. Where would we get the money to make this trip? High schools then did not have much in the way of resources for too many extra-curricular activities like this, but Mr. Maynard was not deterred. He presented our case to the town and they responded. The money poured in, and we were on our way. Who would have ever thought that a bunch of kids from a little high school in a dusty little cowtown would be performing in a national music contest?

It was a great trip! We met the Globe bunch and went on our way. We got to Fresno and we performed — boy, did we ever. I don't mind telling you that I was scared; I was so scared that my mouth was full of cotton and my knees shook. Here were kids from all over the West, and our judges were well-known music educators from everywhere. Five of us produced a brass quartet, a boys' quartet, and three solos. I almost blew my solo, but did manage to get an "Excellent" rating. Our brass quartet got an "Excellent," also, as did our other two soloists, Hardy Kirby on the trumpet and Bill Ewing with a solo bass. Our boys' quartet received the only "Superior" rating given for this type of group. We all felt we had done well, and Delight Maynard was delighted. The Globe kids did well, but not as well as us. We were overwhelmed — those ratings were darned good, especially in the nationals.

We came home to a hero's welcome. We were the toast of the town, asked to perform everywhere.

But what can you do for an encore? We played well my senior year, but there just wasn't the money, and other conflicts of scheduling occurred, so we didn't go to the nationals that year. It is something I will always regret.

Some of us participated in all-state bands and all-state orchestras held in Tucson at the University of Arizona. Those who went were given music to practice, and then we went to Tucson in the early spring. There was always a well-known conductor who directed us. We would try out, individually, for our particular chair in our particular section. I was playing solo trumpet and found myself competing for first chair with boys from Globe and Miami. We made lasting friendships that I still enjoy today.

One of our conductors was Dr. Glenn Bainum of Northwestern University. He was something! When we would "blow it" some way or do something he didn't like, he wouldn't stop us. He would just sit down on the podium and hold his head until we just finally stopped playing. Then he would get up slowly and scold us in a manner such as this: "You people sound like an Italian Army band when they're getting the hell kicked out of them by a bunch of natives." Very tender words, but he got results. When the big night came around, some two hundred and fifty musicians appeared in concert and on national radio.

I had fun with my music. We were most fortunate to have teachers, parents, and friends who believed in us and convinced us that we could do those things we could have only dreamed of.

Then there were sports. We lived for football, basketball, baseball, track, tennis, and even golf. Can you imagine playing golf down that way in those days? In the first place, a blade of grass was about as scarce as you can imagine, and, secondly, to be involved in the sophisticated game of golf in that cowboy town was just about unthinkable — but we had a golf team. Granted, it only lasted a couple of years, but we played. The course was across the railroad tracks on the road out to Dos Cabezas. It was a nine-hole monstrosity that had sand greens. When you hit out in the rough, you were out in the cactus, tumbleweeds, and yucca. There wasn't a sign of a tree on that course or anywhere close. (Nowadays they have two golf courses in that town — I can't believe it.) Nothing much of note ever happened with our golfers except that we did win one tournament.

But I forgot to mention that the second hole paralleled the old graveyard. The old Boothill Cemetery had been there as long as Willcox had, and it really was a shame that the graves had fallen into disrepair and were overgrown with weeds. Well, one day we were out playing golf at this grandiose second hole. If you sliced your drive, you ended up out there among the graves. Well, one of the boys hit his drive right into the middle of the cemetery. The rest of us played our second shot, then waited for him to find his ball and shoot. As we watched him wandering around looking for his ball, he suddenly disappeared! One of the graves had sunken in clear to the bottom. Have you ever heard that old joke about the guy who fell into a grave and couldn't get out, but then he heard a voice and got out right quick? Well, this boy did just the same, only he didn't hear a voice. In fact, as I remember, he was coming out of that hole before he ever hit bottom. Shook him up so much that he quit the golf game that day.

I've seen golf courses recently with beautiful greens and fairways — sure a far cry from the Willcox Municipal of the 1930s.

Football was the big thing, and you weren't much of a man if you didn't play football. That was the code of the school then; sports were the main activity. We could just barely get about thirty to thirty-three boys out — at least we could hold a scrimmage. You bet, we played eleven-man football. No six- or eight-man for us. I don't think they'd even invented those kinds of games then.

Our colors were red and black. When I first started, our coach was C. D. Miller. I can't remember him too well, because I only played for him one year (*played* is a misnomer, *sat on the bench* is better). We went out to the locker room about 2:30 in the afternoon, put on our practice uniforms, and went out to the field directly in back of the school. First was calisthenics, and then down to the real business of knocking heads. I was a sophomore and weighed at least 150 pounds wringing wet, and everyone was bigger than I was. I was always battered and bruised, but it was worth it. Listen, you were a hero if you went out for football, you were the elite of the school. And you never had to worry about your ability or about getting cut from the squad. The coach was just happy to have as many bodies as he could get out there. In all fairness, though, I must add that a number of boys in school couldn't participate in sports because they had to be home for the ranch or farm chores, and the bus left early.

We usually played our games on Friday afternoon, and when we played at home, groups of bleachers were put up along the field in back of the school. The entire town closed down for the event. You couldn't buy a thing in that town when a game was on. Back then, you didn't have such things as class triple "A" or "B" — you just played whoever was closest. Our conference was Clifton, Pima, Tombstone, Douglas, Bisbee, sometimes Nogales, Tucson High, and occasionally Lordsburg, New Mexico.

Red and Black — Fight! Fight!

At least we had grass on our field, as did a few other schools where we played, but many didn't. Clifton was nothing but a dust bowl, and in Miami we played on a slag dump. In Tombstone, we played on a rocky sloping hill, and if someone kicked the ball out-of-bounds on one side, it rolled down into a gully. The game was stopped while someone ran down and got it. We only had two balls — one to practice with and one to play with — very precious commodities.

I played center, and we played the "Pop Warner Double Wing" or the "Short Punt" formation, no fancy "T" or "slot T" or "Wishbone." The quarterback stood several feet behind the line in both formations, so you had to look back through your legs and center the ball to him. If you think we weren't vulnerable to getting clobbered by that guard right across the line, you better believe it. And I got clobbered! I liked to play defense, that was my deal. I played linebacker, so I got into a good bit of the action.

You should have seen us, the Willcox Cowboys, take the field. What a resplendent sight. We wore black helmets, black shirts with red numerals outlined in white stitching, black pants, black and red socks, and black shoes. The material was some kind of shiny satin; we were beautiful! The helmets, in those days, had no masks or covering of any kind over the face, so your face was exposed, and my face, mouth, and teeth took a beating.

Mother wouldn't come to the games. She just knew I was going to get hurt, so Friday afternoon's glories completely escaped her. Dad came, along with practically everyone else in town, and I can still see him walking up and down the sidelines following the play. He didn't sit down much, but then, he wasn't the only one. Many of the parents did the same thing. I can hear Hattie Gardner yelling along the side, also (her boys, Lee and Ray, played), and she was as good as the rest of the cheering section put together.

In my junior and senior years we had a new coach, Ken Pearson, assisted by Joe Wisdom. These two left no doubt in our minds where the authority came from — and the discipline. They worked our tails off, literally. Their word was law; not that the former coaches didn't go after the same results, but these two put some real teeth in it.

A coach, back then, was a man to listen to, to respect and to obey to the letter. If he told you to be in bed at nine o'clock, you knew you were to be in bed. You ate the right kinds of food and you followed his instructions to the letter. I really had to toe the mark because the coach lived in a very nice apartment right in back of our house that we had fixed up to rent. There was not about to be any rule-breaking by me.

Our team wasn't exactly a world beater, but we did achieve some sort of success, and we always knew that the other team knew they had been in a ball game after playing us. We had a pretty rough and tough bunch. We humiliated Bisbee on their own field, and I don't think they came out of that shocker for years — getting beaten by upstart Willcox. Probably the greatest highlight was in my senior year when we played Lordsburg, New Mexico, on their field. Their team had already tucked away the state championship of New Mexico. We were slated to lose. But we went over there and surprised them and ourselves, too, by proceeding to "stomp 'em."

Since I played center (Number "33"), I had to center the ball back. None of this just handing it to the quarterback. When I was in there I usually ended up on the seat of my pants with the opposing guard running right over me. Lee Gardner played left guard, and he pulled on nearly every play and led interference. But if things just were too tough trying to handle that nose guard, I'd tell Joe Anaya, our quarterback, to let Lee stay in the line for a few plays and block him. Lee was just plain mean. Not dirty — no way. But he'd stay in there about three or four plays, and then I was all set, no more problems across the line. Lee was about six feet three inches and about two hundred twenty pounds.

Basketball was about the same when it came to what schools were played, except that we did play teams like St. David and Benson in addition to the others. They didn't play football, but they did play basketball, and they were always good. All games were played at night, and the gyms were packed. Our little gym had standing room only. When the action got swift, fast, and furious, it wasn't hard for the crowd to get into the thick of the fray. I can remember, many times, the game being called, and we would stand out on the court and watch some of the best free-for-alls you have ever seen. I suppose it just was not in the cards to get the townspeople of Benson and Willcox and others that close together in a gymnasium. The local constable and deputy sheriff would finally restore order, and then on with the game.

Again, the facilities we played in left a lot to be desired. In our gym the baskets were right next to the walls. Big wrestling mats were draped on the wall under the basket because you always slammed into the wall going into the basket. In Benson, where their gym doubled as an auditorium, you could go driving for the basket, leap into the air, come down and drape yourself right over the stage. In Tombstone the crowd sat in a balcony along one side of the gym. If things didn't go their way, we, the opposition, got showered with cups, water, Coke, paper, and anything else they could get their hands on — never anything too dangerous, but we got the message. At Bisbee, we played at the gym in the old high school, and the crowd sat right down next to the court. It wasn't too unusual to suddenly get tripped going down the court. It was always dangerous to throw the ball inbounds, because you had to stand right there in front of them. Anything could happen, and it often did.

Franklin Jordan and Ken Pearson were our basketball coaches. Jordan was more of a disciplinarian than our other coaches. He stood for absolutely no nonsense. We practiced, practiced, practiced. Many a night I didn't get home until after dark to eat, but I loved it. No doubt about it, basketball and baseball were my favorites back then. Our team was pretty successful and we won our share. Games were slow, then, compared to the games nowadays. Until my senior year you had to come back and jump center after each score, so games were won by scores like 28 to 23, or 19 to 15. Needless to say, you played for the good shot.

I played forward. I was about five feet ten inches and weighed in during my last year at about 160 pounds. I was "high point man" many times, with at least eight or ten points — how about that!

Baseball was spring, the trees budding, balmy days, and the crack of bat and ball on the dusty field in back of the grade school. Jordan was coach here, too. I played second base and got so I could hit pretty well. We played just about the same teams as for the other sports, and we were pretty good.

I could go on and on about all the things we did at that little school, but I would never finish. It was fun, surely the best time a young person will experience. The days were pretty much carefree, even though we did take ourselves pretty seriously and we did have those "serious" problems to meet. I wish I had those kinds of problems these days.

We held our teachers in respect, and regarded them with esteem and real affection. They were doing something for us, and we were brought up in our homes that this was the way to act toward them. As I've said, the town's social life swirled around the school — athletic events, school plays, band and glee club concerts, speech contests — just anything and everything brought out the town. We had special assemblies, and sometimes, not too often, we even got a pretty good program to come. We had travelogs, clown and magician acts, and some of the most boring speakers I have ever heard — but they were events in that little town.

I've only touched lightly on the happenings at Willcox High in my time; to go into further detail would keep us going forever. I think I have brought you some insight into the life of our town and school then. It was fun, as I said, but serious things were happening. The dark clouds of war were looming bigger and bigger. We kids were at first just mildly curious, reading about Hitler, Tojo, and the rest, passing over it lightly and worrying only about the next ball game or dance.

I don't want to give you the impression that, down there in that remote part of the world, we were not aware of world affairs or concerned about them, because we were. Our teachers had instilled in us that we were very much a part of these great United States and, in turn, were very much a part of the world.

We kids in that school were well-versed on current affairs, thanks to teachers like Franklin Jordan. We discussed, argued, and fought over elections and issues. We knew the names and the performances of U.S. and world leaders. I once wrote an essay, submitted to the State Department in Washington, that even gained national recognition. (I had hoped to get a scholarship out of it to study abroad but just missed.) Anyway, you get my point — we were informed and we were concerned, although it all seemed so far away.

But the whole thing came down to reality when the thirty-three students in our class graduated. The Baptist minister at our Baccalaureate service proceeded to point to us boys sitting there on the stage and announced that many of us might never go much further in life. He was referring to the war, of course. This so upset and enraged the townspeople that he would dare bring this up at a time like that, that this gentleman was almost run out of town. But his prophecy became a reality, and a number of those boys — friends of mine that I had deep affection for — never returned to Willcox and never saw their dreams realized.

As I walked to the podium to receive my diploma, Ernest Browning, President of the school board, said as he handed it to me, "Bob, if you perform in life as you do on the baseball field, you can only be a tremendous success." I did some serious thinking. I thought of my friends, my teachers, all of the things I had had the opportunity to do, and I was certainly more than thankful that I had lived those days in that little town. I was sad, at the same time, because it was all over. Back in my mind was the knowledge, neatly tucked away in some little cranny, that our world would never be the same and that future generations in Willcox would not see nor know the things we had known.

Our whole world never got over World War II, and I'm sure it never will. It started our country and the world on a whole new line of thinking. Sure, there's been a lot of progress, new technology, new innovations that make life easier. But to a pre-World War II graduate of Willcox High, a whole way of life — a good way — has been lost to us. But we aren't the losers, it's the young people today. I'm sure they don't think so, or maybe they do, as they hear some of us "old goats" talking about our day.

I certainly do not advocate returning to the "good old days," but I am sure in favor of resurrecting those values, morals, and basics that give life a meaning and purpose and that have been lost in the shuffle today.

Fun, Games, and Girls

I HOPE THAT I haven't portrayed myself, the young people, and the town folks as always upstanding, righteous, and beyond reproach in our everyday lives. That would be misrepresentation at its worst. We had fun and got into a little mischief, and some of the grown-ups did some things that landed them in the lock-up from time to time.

I don't want to leave an impression that there wasn't any hanky-panky and other shenanigans going on. We had our good W. C. T. U., the local temperance group from the churches, and we had good church-goers who looked down on some of the goings-on with great distaste and disgust. By and large, we kids were made to realize that we would conduct ourselves in an upstanding manner or there would be dire consequences. I am certainly not one who says that the morals in a small town are any better or any worse than in a larger one. But as a young man growing up in Willcox, I knew that I couldn't get away with much, even had I wanted to, because everyone knew you and was aware of what you were up to, and they had no compunctions about going to your folks with any misdeeds. In other words, it was very difficult to lose yourself in a small town. I know that the realization that we could very easily get caught made us lead pretty straight-laced lives.

And we had a different "bringing-up" then than now. I know there are arguments pro and con about the narrow attitudes of parents, teachers, and townspeople then, but as I reflect on those days and see the lack of discipline and morals condoned today, I wouldn't trade my growing-up period with any youngsters today. In fact, I feel sorry for most of them, because I see a complete lack of direction for most these days that certainly wasn't our lot. For the most part, parents were strict, teachers were strict, and the townspeople got into the act, also. They were concerned about us younger ones, and they took it upon themselves to take us to task if need be. Yet they were also quick to support and to help if the need arose. The whole town took a great interest in its young people. This is natural in small towns, even today.

We had our rascals, but most of the mischief was not of serious consequence. The Halloween pranks were really tricks. When I was just starting high school, one of those wild groups got into the high school one night and pushed and shoved a good-sized calf up on the balcony and left it. When school convened the next day, the principal and custodian had one heck of a time getting the animal down. And the calf hadn't been too dainty in its manners. The high school was immediately called into general assembly, and we were sermonized at great length on "this terrible deed." We soaped cars and we whitewashed fences. I happened to participate in the demise of an outhouse in traditional fashion. We approached the structure very quietly and cautiously, then rushed in and pushed it over, all the way over. What we hadn't anticipated was that there was a Mexican gentleman in there. We learned a lot of Mexican cusswords that night. Man, did we run from there!

I only remember one instance when a teacher was shown disrespect or had jokes played on him. Unfortunately, we did have a teacher who only lasted one year teaching manual arts. He was definitely a sissified type. Manual arts was a class in woodworking and other crafts. The shop was in the basement of the building and was equipped with all types of power tools such as band-saws and circular saws. The gentleman had the misfortune of having all of the rowdies in his afternoon class, and they were seniors. This bunch was one year ahead of me. What occurred took hours of work and all kinds of ingenuity to accomplish. What if all this energy had been expended in worthwhile activity, what could have been done? But then . . . well, these clowns sneaked into the shop one night — a plain case of breaking and entering — and they rewired and rearranged all the tools in the place. The next day, when class took up in the morning, the students dutifully took their places by their machines. Switches were thrown, and all hell broke loose. Fire flew in all directions, the switch on the drill press started a saw, a switch on a saw started something else, and nothing could be stopped, or so it seemed. Smoke poured out of the shop and pandemonium reigned. The power in the entire high school had to be turned off and the local electrician called in to work well into the night to restore order. Again we went to the auditorium for a lecture. We all knew who did it, but there were no "stoolies" that day.

The final *coup-de-grace* came when this same group appeared early one morning and found the manual arts teacher in his little glassed-in office in the shop. They proceeded to take a soldering iron to solder and close up the keyhole in his door. He had locked the door and now he couldn't get out. They took off, and wouldn't you know it, it was "Senior Ditch Day" and Friday at that, and they were long gone. Finally, after a lot of yelling and beating on the door, the teacher was heard and his rescue was made. The culprits figured that the weekend would pass and things would cool down. But they didn't, and this group was to be found performing janitorial duties the rest of the year, seniors or not.

I could go on with other stories of such type, but, really, there wasn't much of this type of activity. We were too darned busy. I hear the kids today complaining about having nothing to do. That wasn't the case with us. I blame parents and society today for this. You see, we all had jobs when we were old enough to be in high school. We worked in the stores, mowed lawns, helped out with the family business, or whatever. And we had chores to do at home. There just wasn't any time to get into trouble, with our school activities and all this, too. Kids today just can't find the jobs like we could, and then television has reared its time-consuming head.

In addition, we didn't have to look very far for entertainment, nor did we spend a lot of money. If we had any free time, we got our tennis racquets and got into some good games of tennis on the high school courts, both boys and girls. Many a Saturday or Sunday afternoon, a bunch of us got an old football and played some rough games of touch football on the high school front lawn — again, both boys and girls. We could always find something to do, and we had fun.

Now, here's the part you've been waiting for — girls and sex! But I am afraid it's going to be pretty disappointing if you're looking for some wild stories. Don't get me wrong, we kids in high school there were just as normal as any others, and we got interested in girls and the girls got interested in us, all in due course. And I know that we had some pretty torrid love-affairs going on. But we were all busy, and almost all of our crowd were on the naive side when it came to the opposite sex. We sure didn't think of girls as "soft boys," but one might have thought so the way we mixed and mingled. The girls got out and played all the sports right along with us boys, and they were, for the most part, just part of the gang. From time to time, there'd be a couple here or a couple there that would pair off for an occasional date, but the whole deal was a temporary one.

We did have some "steadies," but these were few and far between, and as I remember, these couples were of the older crowd. I just cannot remember many of our bunch getting that involved. What's also a strange thing is that nearly all of the "steadies" I knew went on to get married. It must have been true love.

Nope, we just didn't have time to get into the love scene. Sure, there may have been other factors, too, but I'm sure this was mainly the case.

The grass is always greener on the other side of the fence. We boys (but not so much the girls) were always interested in the girls from other schools. We had plenty of opportunity to meet them, too. After all the ball games of any kind, we threw a dance for the visiting team and their rooters. And the same happened when we went out of town to play. A lot of "calf-eyes" were thrown around, and a lot of flirting took place. We boys would eye the stag line and maybe, just maybe, get a dance or two, but mainly we did a lot of looking, smiling, and "checking our feet" every so often, to see if they were still there. Still in all, we did meet some very nice girls, and in some of the towns closer to home we even got to the point of correspondence. But that, too, wasn't of much consequence.

No sir, you couldn't say that we boys were the smooth, debonair Casanovas we would like to have been or thought we were. At dances, the boys and girls got in some "good licks." All the school dances and the community dances were well attended. All the families came, and the old folks and some of the little kids were there and did some "rug-cuttin'." Those dances were something! I was usually playing for one, if not in Willcox, then somewhere else. We even had a jukebox in the high school auditorium and, once a week, at noon, we could go up there and turn it on (no money needed, just punch your selection) and we danced for about an hour.

I only remember one girl as a true favorite of mine in Willcox. Girls were just buddies to me. Maybe I didn't fascinate them too much either, so I just never got in much dating except for the big date I mentioned before to the prom with Jean Divelbess.

I can only think of one real girlfriend I had while in high school, and that was a long distance romance if there ever was one. Bowie was down the road (a dirt one, at that, even though it was the main highway) some twenty-five miles to the east of us. It was a railroad town, pure and simple. There was a Southern Pacific hotel and restaurant, a big roundhouse, and all types of facilities for the railroad. There was a lot of traffic so all of these had to be there. It was a big junction and a stopping-off point for freight and passengers taking the spur up to Safford and the Globe-Miami area. It seemed that all of the railroaders there had daughters. I never saw a town that had so many girls in ratio to boys. The boys in that high school had their pick, but it seemed that the girls were checking out the greener pastures of Willcox, because a lot of the Bowie girls got teamed up and paired off with Willcox boys at the dances and church functions.

One of my very closest friends then was Bill Cook. Bill was a prize guy, and we did a lot together. His dad was Tay Cook, who, along with his mother, (Bill's grandmother) and his brother, Mark, owned and operated the Cook Cattle Company (the old Munk Ranch). At that time, that ranch was one of the largest around. The main ranch house was about five miles from Bowie, at the foot of some low hills north of the road heading into Bowie. The ranch spread out toward the Dos Cabezas to the south and then west and north up into and around the lower part of the Grahams. I spent many a weekend and many weeks in the summers out there. Those were working visits. You see, if you ever went out to a ranch to visit, you just naturally fell into all the work and the chores, too. Tay Cook, for some reason, called me Oscar. I saw him the other day and he still calls me Oscar. I have no idea where he got that. But anyway, Bill and I got "sweet" on two of

Fort Bowie, Arizona, 1894 (COURTESY "ARIZONA RANGE NEWS," WILLCOX)

the "Belles of Bowie." Bill dated Billie Jean Bouck and I paired off with Shirley (Pinky) Dillon. Now, when I say we were dating these girls, our dates were not like any dates you've ever heard of.

There was a local schoolteacher in Bowie, a single lady, who was nice enough to load a bunch of those girls in her car and bring them to Willcox to the movies. The theater in Bowie only held one show a week, so this was a big excursion to the big city on Sunday afternoon for the matinee. There we would meet and sit together. Very little privacy. Pinky and I would be surrounded by Bill, Billie Jean, and the rest of the girls, but at least I got to see her and sit next to her, and maybe even hold hands. How about that! Pretty wild affair. After the movie, we would go next door to the Sweet Shop for a Coke, and then the girls would pile in the car and head for home. This same action occurred when the girls came to Willcox for a dance. We met them inside, danced, and then they headed home. If it sounds like I was disappointed with this arrangement — well, I was, and so were Bill and the other fellows who were lucky enough to "squire" one of these girls. All these girls were cute and fun to be with.

We did have our times to be alone. As you might have suspected, however, nothing more occurred than did when we were well-chaperoned. We boys just weren't too "swift" in those days. On those weekends that I was out at the Cook Ranch with Bill, working my head off, the elder Cooks, Tay and Ruth (Bill's parents), went into town to visit Mother Cook. This was a weekend ritual. As soon as the car was out of sight, Bill and I rushed up on the little hill in back of the house and piled all types of wood, greenery, and anything that would burn. We would get a big bonfire going and the smoke would billow skyward. We had it prearranged that the girls in Bowie would watch our way with binoculars. When they saw smoke, they'd pile into Billie Jean's car and come visit us.

Now, Mrs. Cook knew what was going on, so there would be a freshly-made freezer of ice cream in the well-house and a freshly-baked cake in the kitchen oven. We would take the girls horseback riding, sit around and listen to records, and do all those proper activities — and, of course, eat. There was never any hanky-panky or even an attempt made; don't think Bill and I knew enough about girls to have even started anything. And I know that if we had, we would most certainly have gotten our faces slapped.

On one such visit from the Bowie girls, disaster struck. Bill's folks got ready and piled into the car. We waited the proper amount of time; the coast was clear. We rushed up on the hill and got the fire going, standing to watch it burn. The fire burned down and we sauntered off down the hill, awaiting the girls. We hadn't been down there but a few minutes when we looked back up the hill and saw the whole top of the mountain on fire. Our signal fire had gotten out of control, and was it ever going! Bill and I rushed up there with shovels and axes and went to work to stem the fire. The girls came and they helped. That blasted fire burned down the whole mountain, and we just barely saved the corrals from catching it. We worked until after dark, and then the girls went home. We were all dirty and exhausted. Boy, did we dread the return of the folks from Willcox. We went to bed knowing that Bill's dad wouldn't be able to see anything until morning and hoping that maybe he wouldn't be too angry. But it wasn't to be. About four-thirty, in came Tay to get us going. When he left the room to go outside, we sat there trembling in our boots. In the first light of day he saw the damage. We heard a tremendous bellowing and yelling. I can't repeat what was said here, except the last line, which went like this, "Who the hell was the smart aleck dumbbells who burned this mountain?" He knew, and we were soon confronted. After chewing us out pretty good, and I mean professionally, he worked us that day until we couldn't put one foot in front of the other. In fact, we were in the doghouse the rest of the summer over that.

So, there you have it, the tale of the great love affair. I really did like Pinky and we remained friends for many years after that. After graduation, we saw each other just once, and then she moved to California. The railroad was shutting down Bowie's big operations. I kept in touch with her, in a manner of speaking. We exchanged a few letters while I was in the service, and when I was released from the Navy at Terminal Island, I contacted her and her folks. She came to see me go through the ceremony of leaving the service, and I returned to her home to enjoy a fine supper with her and her folks. I'm sure now that, at that time, things could have gotten much more serious, but I was returning to school and I was ready to get going and get to it. I heard that she married a fine young man several years later who was somehow involved in the aviation business. Whoever he is, he got himself one fine girl. She really was a sweetheart.

I cannot leave this subject without telling of the good times I spent at the Cook Ranch, irrespective of the girls. I really enjoyed my trips out there. I learned to ride, do a little roping, and, in general, got firsthand acquaintance with ranch work. The fact that I was a guest didn't count for anything as far as Tay Cook was concerned. If you were there, you worked. And he didn't give any consideration to the time that we struggled in from the dances or movies. Around four or four-thirty he was in the bedroom, turning on the lights, booting us out of the sack. We'd gulp down a big ice-cold glass of milk and go out to the corrals for the first chores — milking, watering the stock in the corrals, any feeding that needed to be done — until breakfast was ready. Then Bill and I would go out to the corral, get one of the horses left for the purpose, and ride double into the horse trap to bring in the horses that would be ridden that day. Then it was down to the serious work ahead. We might haul water (one does a lot of that in this country), fix fence, brand (in season), or be midwife at calving time. Herefords are notorious for having a hard time dropping their calves. We rode at this time to doctor the calves, especially for worms.

Believe it or not, the most fun times were those that Bill and I and the old Mexican cook would ride up to a line cabin high in the mountains to cover the upper range. We took the pack mule along with our supplies, and we might be up there for several weeks at a time. Tay would ride in and resupply us from time to time if the work took longer than usual. It was beautiful up there. At night we would sit in front of the cabin and visit, and we could see off in the distance the lights of Bowie and once in a while the lights of a car along the highway (it wasn't too heavily traveled in those days). The work was hard, but we had fun doing it. The food was about as you would expect. For breakfast, we always had beans; our cook always had a big pot of them on the stove. We had bacon, ham, or beefsteak, and *huevos rancheros* (eggs scrambled with onion, chilis, and other spices), sourdough biscuits, and coffee. (When I heard a guy complaining about the coffee in the Navy one day, I told him to enjoy it. Our Mexican cook kept a big pot on the stove, never pouring out the grounds from one day to the next until the pot was so full of grounds that it was virtually impossible to make any coffee to drink. After a few days, that was real "tar." So, Navy coffee was a breeze for me.)

When I wasn't tied up with some kind of music contest or involved in some kind of sports, my weekends were busy. I worked in two different grocery stores as a clerk, shelving stock and delivering groceries. People would call in their orders and I would fill them, load the food in the store truck, and take it to the customer's house. I learned a lot about people, their buying habits and their credit habits. Just about all buying then was on credit. You charged your groceries and paid by the month or on some other prearranged schedule. It was quite revealing.

As with the weekends I spent out at the Cook Ranch, I had another home away from home. Many a day I spent in Dos Cabezas with the Kirbys. Mrs. Kirby, like Ruth Cook, was like another mother to me. She owned and operated the family general store in Dos Cabezas, which had been going since the town had started. Mr. Kirby had passed away many years before, and Mrs. Kirby carried it on. Living at home back then were Hardy, a year older than I; Lynn, my age; and Robert, who was in grade school and then in high school my last year. There were older children who were married and gone. I can still see Mrs. Kirby now, with her beautiful white hair piled high upon her head, an infectious grin, and a motherly countenance.

The Dos Cabezas Mountains were a smaller range of the valley, and Willcox sat right at the foot of their western end. To get to the little town of Dos Cabezas, you took a dirt road (now paved) east alongside the mountain for seven to eight miles, and then the road curved up into the mountains themselves. You traveled into a wide pass with low-lying foothills to your right (east) and the high ranges and the peaks to your left (west) for about three miles and then, all of sudden, you were in the little village itself.

When we first moved to Willcox, Dos Cabezas was very large, but only in regard to the number of buildings and houses in it. At one time it was a large mining town, and many of the mine buildings, the old railroad, and even the roundhouse, mill, and labs were still there. There were houses everywhere, nearly all of them vacant. You see, Dos Cabezas had been the main town and mill-site for the mine at Mascot. You could stand in the main street, looking up toward the peaks, and follow with your eye the huge overhead tramway, still in place, all the way up to the now-abandoned town of Mascot. Mascot was a large town, too, as ghost towns go. Probably several hundred people still lived in Dos Cabezas at that time. The school was going strong, and all the kids got their grade school education there, then were bused to Willcox for high school. Along the main street were two general stores, a bar and poolroom, and other enterprises that lasted only short times. The old cemetery lay at the edge of town.

Now there are very few buildings left. Most of the houses were moved to Willcox, where people took them, remodeled them, and made them their homes. I loved to go up there — what a place to explore and wander around in. I wish I had had the foresight to pick up some of the old pieces of equipment and the treasures that lay everywhere, turning to rust and dust. To us, these were just "junk." Now, people are selling them, collecting them, and they're worth plenty. But who's to know sometimes?

The Kirbys were just like another family to me, and we had many a fun time. The Kirby house sat on a low slope above the store, a long rectangular house with another little bunkhouse in the back. Several of the kids made that little building their rooms, and that's where I always stayed.

At night we would all gather in the living room. Tiny Hurtado and Dick and Don Thompson would come over. All of us played instruments, and Mrs. Kirby played the piano. We would have a real jam session. Man, those old mountains rocked with some wild music many a night.

The old store was a piece right out of the past. You could buy everything from patent medicines to clothes, and groceries of all kinds. Best of all were the candy jars with all types of hard candy. The old potbellied stove sat in the middle of the floor with the pickle barrel close by. The place was a busy one. The nearby ranchers and the miners that still eked out a bare living working gold, silver, or both claims out in the hills came in for supplies. Fond memories drift in and out of my mind, reliving those wonderful days.

We spent our days helping at the store, but mainly roaming the area in search of whatever. There were many other kids living up there, the Thompson boys, the Miskovich family, and, of course, the Hurtados. The Hurtado ranch house was just across the town and part-way up the hill toward Mascot. We spent a lot of time there. Tiny was one of my best buddies, and I spent several weekends with the Hurtados.

Across the way was the old adobe house where another friend lived, Tom Bean. The house had been the Butterfield Stage depot when that very famous stage line was in operation. We found arrowheads and bullets embedded in the walls, the result of Indian raids. Mr. Bean had to put a stop to us digging in the walls for souvenirs before the walls came down — after all, it was their home.

Well, I hope that I have conveyed to you that my days were full and my life was full. Girls were a definite part of my life, but mostly as friends. Sometimes I felt that I was missing something, but I really wasn't. We all had fun together and did things together, and there was a comradeship that remains today among us all. Once in a while we get together and talk of the old times and realize what a wonderful time and place that was.

And you can see, too, that we were a busy bunch. There was always something to do. These were times that remain as jewels in my life.

And Then There Was Church

ERY PROBABLY the most important part of my growing up was being part and parcel of a Christian home. My parents were devoted to their church and their God. Both of them lived a true Christian life, I mean, they really lived it! So many times that statement is made and it just does not fit, but in my home, it did.

I say these things because my dad and my mother lived their faith with each other, with their children, and, very especially, with others. Our home was one of true affection and true concern for one another, and when I told you a little about my parents, I could not tell of the wonderful things and the thoughtfulness they had for others. My dad, a seriously ill man, and my mother, concerned and helping him, faced Dad's illness and the financial difficulties that went with it. Yet always they had time and resources to help someone else.

I can see my mother picking the beautiful flowers in her garden to take to someone who was ill, or just because she was concerned or thinking of them, and the flowers might be a cheerful note in a drab existence. She also baked and cooked, and people all over town ate cookies, pie, or cake just because she thought it might be nice for them. So it was with all kinds of little gestures on her part. She always found time to visit someone who was ill. People knew that she could always be counted on to help wherever and whenever needed.

Dad was much more quiet about anything he might be doing or might have done for someone else. But I remember many a day that he would come home with a big sack of potatoes or a basket full of corn or vegetables, or some such item. It would turn out that Dad had gone to help a farmer or rancher with a sick cow or horse or had performed some kind of deed that these people felt they had to repay with something.

Even today, many years after Dad has gone, I am still often told by someone of a time of need when my dad responded. I'm sure that even Mother did not know about much of this. I knew that he gave money, over and above any type of charitable drives to which he contributed, to Hazel Johnson, who handled the monies to be distributed to the needy. Dad would just tell Hazel to do with it what she thought best for those who needed it. When Dad died, I went to the local florist to order flowers from the family. The florist told me that for years, my Dad would come in to her shop just before Christmas and order flowers sent to all those in the hospital on Christmas — no card, no nothing — just done to bring a little cheer to these people. She broke down and cried when she told me, no one but she had known, until then. Dad was like that. He was always willing, able, and available to help.

Why did I start this way — you're thinking that I am doing another chapter on my parents. No, that's not it. I mention these things because one day I was sitting at the dinner table and we were all talking and visiting as we always did, and I asked my dad and mother why they were always doing for other people. To me it seemed that they did an awful lot, and there were times that this interfered with my plans. I might need Mother to iron a shirt for me, and she would be out visiting or something, and I would get somewhat peeved. Or Dad just wasn't available when I thought he should be, and I just plain did not understand. And I sure didn't see much reward for all this.

Well, I got the answer, and quickly. The gist of the whole thing, according to them both, was to remind me of what I was supposed to be learning in church — that you did for others. This was a basic premise of Christ's ministry. They reminded me that we do not live in this world by ourselves and we need the fellowship of others and the good feeling of having done something worthwhile. As Dad said, "What else do you really get out of life, unless it's the knowledge that you have served?" They didn't mean this in any manner to be "holier-than-thou." Far from it. They were just trying to explain their actions to me, and the final word from Mother was, "Bob, it's fun to do something for someone. You'll see for yourself. Try it."

Church and church activities were a focal point of my life. Sunday meant Sunday School, church, and, at evening, Epworth League (now known as Methodist Youth Fellowship). Young people reading this today might say, "How boring." We weren't so different, in many ways, from the young today, since oftentimes we felt the same way. The difference, as I see it, was that we really did enjoy most of it, and we had parents who insisted on church attendance as regular routine. As far as my parents were concerned, we kids went, whether or not we wanted to. Nowadays parents won't, by and large, enforce that. Rather than start a hassle, they give in to the youngsters.

I can give a good example of what I mean. One Saturday I played for a dance. Bill Cook attended and, for the one and only time, he was able to get his grandmother's car for the occasion. We made arrangements to take our two Bowie girlfriends home afterward. This was to be a real occasion. After we delivered the girls we would return to Willcox. Bill planned to spend the rest of the night with his grandmother.

The dance ended about one in the morning and we all hurried down to the Red Arrow (an all-night eating place and service station-garage) for a hamburger. We finished there about two and went on our way to Bowie, which was about twenty-five miles away on a dirt road. We delivered the girls about three. Approximately halfway back to Willcox, we had a flat. No problem, we'd just get out the old jack and fix it. But, to our surprise and dismay, there was no jack. Well, what do you do? I'll tell you what we did — we walked. We got back to the Red Arrow just about the time the sun was coming over Dos Cabezas. As we were talking to the mechanic and getting ready to go back for the car with a jack, I saw my dad go by in his car — he was looking for us. Bill called his grandmother, who by this time was up and worried, and Bill and the mechanic decided they could get the car. I went home to be greeted by a very anxious mother. Mother was so relieved to see me that nothing was said, and she put on the biggest, best breakfast for me you ever saw. I don't mind telling you that I dreaded what Dad would say and do when he got back. When he returned, he had seen the car with the flat on the side of the road, but he wasn't angry or perturbed in the least.

Since nothing was said, I went into my room to get ready for a real good sleep. Ho, ho, not to be! Dad came in and in his quiet but very firm manner informed me that it would soon be time for Sunday School and church, and that I would be very conspicuous by my absence. No questions, no arguing — I would just go, and that was that. I went, but I was so sleepy that I went in a fog. After church and after Sunday dinner, I was allowed to go to bed.

Now, the whole affair was not my fault, but no matter, Sunday was the Sabbath. As far as my parents were concerned, it would be observed. Many today would argue that it was ridiculous to make me go, and, I'm sorry to say, most wouldn't have cared, period.

I look back now and am grateful that my parents did discipline us kids to church attendance. It did not make us resentful because all the kids that were Methodist were in attendance, too. This was true of the other denominations in town, also.

We had a lot of fun with church events. On Sunday nights we Epworth Leaguers met in the front room of the parsonage. We always had a good devotional and a lesson and then refreshments. We had recreation times where we played games. And there were the outings. We went on picnics, to summer camps, and we had district meetings, mainly with the Safford and Duncan Methodist Churches. We made many friends at these meetings, and we boys ogled the girls and vice versa. I made a lot of friends who I saw and knew the rest of my life.

In a small town you just didn't get the "topdrawer" ministers. (There's a statement that can get me in trouble.) But that was a fact. We either got the young ones just starting their career or the older ones on their way to retirement. But, in all fairness, in my years there we were pretty lucky and did get some fine men. I'll never forget Reverend Meyers, though. He was young, full of pep, with a good-looking wife, and — horrors! — he drove a baby blue convertible. Well, the staid and solid group in the church were aghast over this — it just wasn't dignified. So the good Reverend started out with two strikes against him, but his enthusiasm, warmth and vitality soon won over even the most hardened critic of his lifestyle. He was informal, he was brash, and we kids fell in love with him. When it came to the kids in church, his motto was, "Let's do something." He was ready to go at the drop of a hat. Most importantly, he made church a fun place. He was the first minister I knew who made us realize that the church was not a place to go to be admonished for our sins and be given "hell-fire and damnation." He taught us that the good Lord was a forgiving Lord and that there was salvation for all of us. And he made us know that our Christian faith was to be enjoyed — there was fun to be had.

Before him, all the ministers had been of the old school. All we heard was that we were doomed if we didn't repent and all of the dire consequences if we were slackers in any way. But Reverend Meyers was a "man of the cloth" giving us an entirely new idea, and a joyful one. At first, again, the older members rebelled. This new approach was hard for them to swallow, but they did, finally, and they loved it. It was a real time of mourning when Reverend Meyers left. He went right to the top, and he is now the senior pastor at one of the largest Methodist churches in the world, in California. We knew there would be no stopping him.

I certainly do not want to put down the other ministers who were there, but this young man completely captivated all of us and gave us a whole new dimension to our Christian faith.

I also don't want to leave you with the impression that we were a very pious, deeply religious group. Far from it. There was too much about our faith that we didn't know or understand. The very devout and deep-thinking young Christians of today have it all over our group when it comes to knowing their Bible and when it comes to a much deeper conviction on each individual's part. But where our group of young people had it all over the youngsters I see today was the complete fellowship, the togetherness, and the real feeling of togetherness with our families. A lot of our participation was forced on us by our parents and by the pressures of living in a time and place where "all *good* children went to church." We felt very put upon at times, but I cannot remember a time that we didn't enjoy church and its activities.

Our little church was a wooden building on a corner about two blocks from my home. The pews inside were wooden, also, and hard. (I never did understand why these older churches were so uncomfortable. Well, yes, I guess I do, too. This would insure making it hard for the sleepers.) The floor sloped from the back toward the front to the altar. Along the front and to your left as you entered the church was a raised area where the choir sat. The piano, later replaced by an organ, was placed between the choir and the altar, just a little to the back. I can see the whole scene now. My mother, in her Sunday finery, playing that piano. Us kids, sitting in our places. Then in came the choir during the singing of the first hymn. They entered from a door at the left rear of the church, and my Dad was among them. He sang many a solo in that church. I can see my sister, when she was still very young, singing solos there, and I can remember sitting in a chair, nervous, sweating, my mouth dry, awaiting the time I would get up and play a trumpet solo. Once I got started, it wasn't too bad, but the anticipation just about killed me.

The Bliss family participated — you better believe it. I wouldn't give all the treasure of the world for my experience with my family in the Christian faith. As I grow older, I appreciate more and more the example set for me by my parents, the ministers, and the members of that little church. Perhaps I have failed miserably to live up to the expectations these people might have had for me and I have not kept faith as I should at times, but it cannot be said that they were at fault. This background left me knowing that there is a power greater than all of us and that this old world and, especially, myself, depend on our Lord and our faith. Today, too many parents haven't got the guts to see to it that their children have this background and this religious experience. It is mainly because they set no example themselves. At least in my time, most people recognized the need for religious upbringing, and the magic word was commitment. Today, that magic word is a rare find among those who do not go to church, and even those who do. It's a sad commentary.

Believe It or Not

EVENTS OCCURRED in the valley that I'm sure many would tend to discount or be hard put to believe all they heard about them. But I have to relate some of them, because they were funny, bizarre, and tragic. I don't want to dwell on the tragic, however — that type of happening is all too prevalent in our world, so I will dwell on the others. We even had an oil well drilled right out of town. A lot of high hopes went right down that well — they hit exactly nothing.

The summer that I worked in the drugstore and had just returned from the service, Dr. Hicks, M. D., arrived to set up his practice in our town. There was no doubt that we needed another doctor; Dr. Wilson, the long-time M. D. there, was more than ready for retirement, and the town was also growing. Dr. Hicks (I cannot for the life of me remember his first name, if, indeed, I ever knew it) arrived right out of the U. S. Navy, where it was said that he had been the senior doctor and surgeon on a hospital ship. We felt very honored that he would pick our town to settle in.

The good doctor set up practice down on Front Street or Railroad Avenue — whatever your choice — in the old George Johnson saloon, which he remodeled into an office and clinic. He seemed to be a very competent man, and he was finally able to get me quiet long enough to take out my tonsils at my ripe old age. They had bothered me for years, but I had fought the inevitable during those years. Doc had a wife and some older children who were not in residence. He went out on the edge of town and built the most lavish and weird monstrosity of a house you have ever seen. It was made of adobe and looked like an old fort, and that's the name that was attached to it — Fort Hicks. I won't try to describe the place for you, you have to see it. It's still there, and now it's a mortuary — very appropriate.

Soon it became very obvious that our fine resident doctor had himself a large problem — he was "on the sauce." I mean, he could put away the booze! When sober, he was a fine medical man, but given some good sippin' whiskey, anything might happen and did.

Unfortunately, his head nurse was one who also took to drinking, so the two worked together quite nicely. At the end of the day, the two of them would close the office, pull the shades, head for the "medicine" cabinet, and get started on some serious drinking.

The word got around pretty quick about this activity. The townspeople were now presented this problem, when they had thought that they had their problem solved when it came to medical attention. Soon there were all kinds of stories going around about the good doctor and his activities, all pretty frightful, if you were to believe much of them. But people needed a doctor and he was it, so his practice flourished, in spite of the situation. Unfortunately, his practice was short-lived. One particular incident was very instrumental in the demise of Dr. Hicks.

One evening the office closed, the drinking started, and the doctor and his nurse had settled in for the daily intake, when the phone rang. It was Mrs. Webb, out at the 76 Ranch, very distraught and almost hysterical. One of her ranch hands was apparently in the throes of a heart attack. Dr. Hicks reassured her and advised her that he and his nurse were on their way.

Now, Dr. Hicks was a man who left no stone unturned, nor did he ever pinch pennies — so he had purchased himself an ambulance, no less. This was really something, for Willcox to be so endowed. He and the nurse, replete with a good supply of bottles (and I don't mean medicine), headed out the old dirt road to the ranch on their mission of mercy. They arrived after, I'm sure, a precarious ride, and as the story goes, they found the patient indeed having a heart attack. The doctor, with the help of others there at the ranch, got the man into the back of the ambulance and headed for Willcox and the clinic.

Mrs. Webb, after several hours of anxious waiting for word, decided to call and check on the condition of her employee. She could find no one. She made repeated calls, only to draw a blank. Something was definitely wrong. She called the local deputy sheriff, who advised her to "sit tight" while he headed on back up the road to see if they had had car trouble or an accident or something. He went all the way out to the ranch and saw no sign of the ambulance or its occupants. Well, now, this really got everybody excited. The deputy put out a call to the highway patrol and reported the missing ambulance. The night wore on, and all concerned were anxious and completely puzzled as to the whereabouts of the three and the vehicle. You just don't have a complete disappearance of this type. Finally the deputy, in a piece of brilliant deduction, headed out through Stockton Pass, in the Grahams, toward Safford. Perhaps, just perhaps, the doctor, knowing his limitations of equipment and facilities in Willcox, had headed for better facilities at the hospital in Safford.

The deputy arrived there about two o'clock in the morning. By checking with the local police, he found that they had indeed seen the ambulance, the doctor, and his nurse, and the pair had proceeded to close every bar in town. But the police had had no idea that there was a patient in the back of that ambulance.

It was obvious, now, what was happening. The doctor and his nurse were "high-flying," and there was no telling where they were or what they were up to. But, what of the poor heart attack victim? It was all-important to find the trio. Frantic calls were made to the highway patrol and to all the local law enforcement agencies in the area. About five in the morning, a local policeman in Lordsburg, New Mexico, picked up one of these calls on his radio. He reported that he had seen the ambulance parked on the main street in Lordsburg just a few minutes before. He rushed to the scene, only to find that it was gone. He roused out the local proprietor of a bar, who informed him that the pair had awakened him and got him to sell them some more booze. He had no idea where they were headed. By this time, the chase had spread to both states.

The story ends with the discovery of the ambulance and its occupants on the highway just outside Bowie about eight o'clock the next day. The doctor and nurse were passed out in the front, and the patient was still in the back, and, "wonder of all wonders," still alive. (As far as I know, that man is alive and well today). The other two were gathered in and taken back to Willcox, but what charges would be preferred? This was really a dilemma. Until and unless the patient charged these two with something, they were free to go home and sleep it off.

No charges were filed, but the Arizona Medical Association finally entered the picture later and suspended our Doctor Hicks for this and other improprieties.

Let me state that Dr. Hicks finally recognized that he needed help and turned himself in to the Navy hospital in San Diego. He was rehabilitated and spent many more useful and productive years as a fine doctor, which he always had been, with the Navy until he retired.

His house remains, much as it was when he lived there. The local residents smile as they go by and state, "There's Fort Hicks."

Another event occurred during the war years that had quite an impact on a group of travelers from the "concrete canyons" of New York City and gave the local residents renewed memories of their "wild, wild past."

In Bowie there was a business enterprise that had, over the years, become a landmark in that little city — Skeet's Tavern and Cafe. "Skeet" Thomas was an ageless diminutive man who had presided over his bar for many, many years. When the war came along, it seemed a good idea to add the cafe to his enterprise. If he had a cafe around in the years prior, I certainly don't remember it. But Skeet was an enterprising man, and his business was on the main street, which was the highway also. Since gas rationing was in effect, the main forms of travel, especially transcontinental travel, were by bus or train. The buses coming through needed a place to stop for rest and for eating, so Skeet got right into the act. Perhaps it was just coincidence that his cafe was begun about this time, but I prefer to believe that he could see the money to be made with this and the tie-up with the bus companies. There's nothing wrong with this, far from it. I mention this because there just had been no cafe around, and now there was.

The bar and cafe were housed in a building that stood in the middle of town. The front was all glass, and you entered through a door a little left of the building center. Down the left side was a bar that stretched the length of the bar area. Regular bar stools enabled you to "belly up to the bar." There were a few tables and chairs out from the bar for those parties so inclined. The rest of the room was the cafe: round tables with four chairs at each and a counter at the right side of the room. The whole scene presented a neat, clean, and attractive place to eat or do a little socializing in.

Sure enough, Skeet's became the bus stop for the big buses going through with their full loads of travelers involved in wartime travel. When the buses stopped, the passengers could have coffee, soft drinks, or regular meals, depending on the time and the circumstances. Most of these stops were made by the "express" buses that carried passengers for long distances, say from New York and Chicago to Los Angeles and San Diego and the like.

One of the main stops was the daily noon meal stop by the express from New York City, and this usually consisted of two large buses traveling together. Now, the scene is set for our little episode.

Across the tracks was a little run-down shack inhabited by two old prospectors. These old birds had been around for years, roaming through the mountains of the area in search of the mother lode with no success. The town just accepted the pair for what they were; no one bothered them and they bothered no one. These two were "bosom pals," and inseparable. At this point in time, they would journey out into the wilderness for weeks, even months at a time, so no one got concerned over their comings and goings. They went out looking for the big find, and when the supplies got low they came home.

They and their old burro walked into town one fall morning and headed right for Skeet's. They had a big thirst, and they were going to "cut the dust" before anything else was tended to. They bellied right up to the bar at the back of the room and proceeded to catch up on their drinking. Their personal appearance — unkempt, unshaven, their dirty clothes filling the air with the reek of unwashed bodies — didn't exactly thrill Skeet too much, who was tending bar that morning. But luckily there were no other customers at the bar or in the cafe. Skeet knew these old boys and he wasn't about to turn them away, but he sure was hoping that they got their drinking done in a hurry and got out before others arrived. This pair wouldn't exactly give the place any "class."

The two old codgers began to down the booze, fast and furiously, and as they proceeded, they began to get argumentive with each other. I guess that living together all those months in the hills had brought out some pent-up emotions and some pet peeves. Pretty quickly they were slapping each other, and it soon looked like a full-fledged fight was in the offing. Skeet tried to simmer 'em down, but to no avail. Finally, these two were at it tooth and toenail and calling each other names that you don't exactly repeat in polite company. The bigger of the two finally knocked the small man off his perch, and that did it. "You dirty old son of a b————, I'm going to the shack to get the gun, and I'm comin' back here to plug ya so full of holes you won't hold no coffee no more," yelled the little man. To which the other replied, "Go get the gun, ya sawed-off little shrimp. See if I care. You can't hit nothin' with it, anyway." He just slouched back, deep in his cups, at that. The little fella staggered out of the bar and disappeared. Well, Skeet wasn't too sure whether or not to get excited about this turn of events, but he decided the old boy would just find a tree and sleep off his booze underneath it.

About fifteen minutes later, up drove two of the big Greyhound express buses from New York City, headed for the West Coast. All these folks piled out of the big buses to find the restrooms and to settle in for a nice noon meal. They barely got seated when, sure enough, here comes the drunk, dirty, enraged and put-upon prospector. And he had a gun with a barrel about a foot long. Into the cafe he staggered. Reeling around, he tried to focus and find his enemy, but all he could see was all of these people. He waved the "hog-leg" around, calling for terror, murder and mayhem, "Where are ya, ya dirty old fool. I'm back and I'm goin' to kill ya, like I said I would. You're hidin', you rat." Well, the sight of this old boy and his gun, shouting threats and bodily harm, completely terrorized the good folks from the big city. If there was a way out, they were going to find it. Finally, since he couldn't see too well, this gunslinger got it in his mind that all these people were shielding his target. Waving the gun around and yelling at the top of his lungs, he ordered them to get up and line up against the wall. He went up and down the line cursing and threatening, but he couldn't find his man. Finally, the old boy over at the bar roused himself out of his stupor long enough to yell to the would-be gunman, "I'm over here, you blind old b————." With that, the little man spotted him, aimed the gun with both hands, and shot him right off the stool. Pandemonium and hysteria broke loose, and the crowd shoved and pushed, screaming and yelling, to any exit they could find. The big shooter, realizing what he had done — probably killed his best friend — ran to his downed buddy, crying that he didn't mean to do it. He gathered the old boy in his arms, crying and sobbing. The cafe had emptied out and, I mean, in a hurry. Old Skeet, when he had seen the old man come in with the gun, had sneaked out the back way to find the town constable.

Well, it turned out that the old prospector was only nicked and not shot seriously. They took him over to the hospital in Safford. He refused to press charges against his old friend.

What of the passengers of the buses? Well, the bus drivers picked up their occupants all over town and down the road for miles. Those people from the big city had had their fill of the Old West, and they were ready to get out of there and never return. I know that the big gunfight in Bowie became a major battle as it was told and recounted years later in Brooklyn, the Bronx, etc. As for the old prospectors, they lived for many years after, continuing their sorties into the mountains, hoping to hit it rich — which they never did.

The old Dry Lake, to put it technically, the Willcox Playa, "the most perfect mirage in the Western Hemisphere," was the bane of the housewife's existence in Willcox. When the south winds blew, the alkali dust came through town in waves and clouds of dust that seeped into every crack and opening. My mother was forever and always dusting, and the main culprit was that big old alkali flat sitting out there south of town. But you could drive around that old flat area from any direction and always be amazed and impressed as you looked out to see what was supposedly the water and the reflections of the trees, shrubbery, and mountains surrounding the old lake. I mentioned previously how when we first arrived we thought we were to live right on the banks of a beautiful lake. This ersatz body of water fooled many a tourist and visitor to the area. I can well remember the residents of Cochise, just south of the lake, telling of tourists stopping and asking for bait and where was the best place to fish. How effective the illusion could be was proven one day during the war.

One fine day, in the summer, the U. S. Navy decided to fly one of their big Martin Mariner seaplanes from San Diego to the East Coast. It seems that this big flying boat would travel the southern route through Corpus Christi, Texas. As they came over the mountains east of Tucson, they developed engine trouble. As the report goes, the pilot attempted all types of maneuvers and various actions to circumvent an entire power failure of the four big engines, but they were losing the battle. It soon was apparent that they would have to bail out. This was a seaplane, certainly not built to land, and they were over very hostile terrain. Just as the pilot and captain were ready to give the order to "hit the silk," one of the crew yelled that he had spotted a body of water up ahead of them. Sure enough, there it was, a beautiful big lake. No one remembered such a lake on any of their maps, but who was to worry about that. They could set this big "boat" right down on that lake, ride it right on in. The order was given, and they descended to make the landing. It wasn't until they were just about down, and already committed, that they realized that the water kept moving away from them, that there wasn't any water nor any lake. But it was too late — they were coming in. It was to their advantage, of course, that the mirage was flat as a piece of glass and just about as slick. The big plane settled right on the alkali and skidded several hundred yards and then, just like slow motion, gently leaned over on one wing. No one was hurt. The crew got out and surveyed the area, and they couldn't believe it. The plane wasn't damaged seriously. As they looked in all directions, they could still see the beautiful water off in the distance, always just off in the distance. They realized how they had been fooled, but let me tell you, they weren't complaining. There may not have been any water there, but the old lake provided a smooth place in a very rough area to set her down. They certainly weren't unhappy about the results — not one bit.

The crew walked over to one of the roads along the banks of the lake and were taken into Willcox. There they informed the Navy what had happened. These boys were able to stay in Willcox for several weeks while a crew came in to repair the plane and put temporary wheels on it so they could fly it out. This they did.

I know that somewhere in this United States are some men who still count among their wartime memories that landing on the lake that wasn't there and the participation in the fellowship and hospitality of my little hometown.

The Strange News

NOT MANY TOWNS of Willcox's size could boast of having a newspaper, but Willcox had a weekly. This piece of journalistic information and advertising hit the streets every Friday. It was and still is called *The Arizona Range News,* and it had been published and distributed in that area since before anyone could remember. It was truly a pioneer paper.

During the days I grew up there, this paper was published, edited, and owned, first by the Fullmers, ranchers from the Sunset District, and later by Mr. and Mrs. D. F. Mellunbruch. Mrs. Mellunbruch was the reporter and the advertising salesperson (as they say today), and Mr. Mellunbruch was the "inside" man, running the linotype and the presses to have that paper out each week. Mr. Fullmer stayed on as the printer. There were local correspondents around the valley in various schools and local communities who contributed to the paper. I have to say that it was a very newsy paper. One could pick up a copy and read about everyone who had shown up in Willcox from some outlying area to do their shopping. The school news was always there, very complete with all sorts of details that you might or might not care a bit about — but nevertheless there, in black and white. If you were somewhat squeamish about having your personal activities and personal business being aired in the paper, forget it! There it would be, as big as life. Mrs. Mellunbruch, I must say, had a nose for news, and some said, "too big a nose, and it was many times in the wrong place." We all knew what everyone else was up to, whether they liked it or not.

Mrs. M. also editorialized on this subject and that. Oftentimes one would wonder why or how some of the subjects ever saw the light of day. Most of these magnificent pieces of writing caused several responses: a ho-hum attitude, a large belly laugh, or just plain downright anger. I can't remember any other reaction on the part of the local populace.

It sounds like the paper was not exactly what the reader had in mind as a local newspaper. And there was a lot of criticism, but still, everyone had their copy each week and read it avidly, from cover to cover.

I think that it is quite an achievement that Willcox had this paper. When I think of the population of the town and the surrounding area in those days, I know that the Mellunbruchs and Fullmers supplemented their income by printing all types of other items in order to keep the little paper going. They printed stationery, office forms, cards, and so on. They provided quite a service, over and above the reporting of news.

I could go into monumental detail on some of the stories and items that appeared from time to time, but there would be no stopping place.

When I went to the Navy in World War II, my mother saw to it that I received the paper. I could hardly wait for that small rolled-up piece of paper to show up in my mail. I would sit down right there and read it from cover to cover, becoming very nostalgic and just a little bit homesick. That paper meant almost as much to me as any letter I could have ever received. From the time I received a copy until the next arrived, I would read and reread it many times.

Everyone in town referred to the paper as the "Strange News" because of the play on words and because some of the strangest news you could imagine showed up each week. To an outsider, especially some of the big-city folk, the paper was a riot. When I was on the aircraft carrier and the paper came, I would read it the first time and then I would post a sign-up sheet outside my door for all hands to sign for their turn to read the funny little newspaper from Willcox. My shipmates from every part of the country looked forward to reading that paper almost as much as I did. They would go through it and laugh their heads off at some of the articles, and then some item or two would bring them back to a more serious feeling. Many of them came from large cities and could not even imagine a paper like this one. Many others came from towns very much like Willcox but never received a paper. So I'm sure that this bit of homespun news took them back across the miles to their own hometowns.

I do have to mention one story in particular that was indicative of the type of news and the importance given by the editorial staff. It appeared in an issue while I was in the service, and for years I saved that piece, until I lost it somewhere. There was an older gentleman in our town who had by no means become a "success" in any manner, shape, or form. In fact, he was more readily identified as the town loafer, and he might have also had a title referring to his activities in the local bars. He was a nice gentle fellow who was content with his lot, meager as that was. I think his greatest ambition, to this point, was to just roam around town, visit with his old cronies, and stay out of the rain and the hot sun, as the case might be. Ambition just wasn't in his vocabulary.

But along came the war, and people were asked to do their part. Well, out at the south end of the Dry Lake, the Army Air Corps decided they would put in a bombing range for the boys at Davis-Monthan field and at the base in Douglas to practice on. So a number of barracks and other installations were constructed. *The Arizona Range News,* in a tremendous "scoop" and with great editorial

One of the first oil wells drilled in Arizona, just outside Willcox,
by Loy Turbeville and friends (COURTESY LOY TURBEVILLE)

aplomb, hit the street with a story of a local man who had, overnight, become a "success." Yes sir, our local town ne'er-do-well had his picture on the front page. An article worthy of a tycoon or statesman portrayed a story of overnight success and a future bright with recognition and financial gain. This gentleman, according to the article, after years of solid attempts to arrive at this pinnacle, had somehow been selected as the contractor with the U. S. Army Corps to construct some very necessary additions to the bombing range base. Yes sir, he was to build the outhouses on the base, and they would be two-holers. According to the article, these would be a "deluxe" type of outhouse and would require innovative design and oustanding construction techniques. In reading this, one would have thought

97

that you were dealing with a J. Paul Getty or other type of magnate had you been unfamiliar with the gentleman who was the subject of the story. But knowing his background made the whole thing hilarious. Just another example of the journalistic abilities of the staff of the "Strange News."

Seriously, though, the little paper was a tremendous asset to the town and the area around it. Sure, we had our laughs over various news items and articles such as this one, but we wouldn't have missed an edition for anything. For one thing, everyone got their name in print, sooner or later. If you did anything, even in just your everyday living, you would make the paper.

The paper still comes out today and, nowadays, it is a more cosmopolitan paper. It does its usual great job in reporting the news, and the townspeople look forward to the end of the week when the next edition will be out. The present publishers are well-versed in their profession — nothing like the days I have been talking about. The Mellunbruchs were good people, but their regime came to an end some years ago when they were divorced. Mrs. M. ran the paper for a while but soon decided that her career could only be furthered in a metropolitan area. She sold the paper to the present owners and left for California.

My only regret is that I could not have foreseen this day, when it would be something to go back through some of the old editions of that paper. But I never did save them. Even before my time in the valley, the paper was being printed, and the old stories are a treasure trove of history in the area.

Well, we all called it the "Strange News," and it sure did offer some very strange bits of information. But we were very fortunate to have that paper in our midst, just as I'm sure the people there feel about it today.

Epilogue

WELL, THERE YOU HAVE IT. The joys, sorrows, victories, disappointments — the whole gamut. My family and I experienced it all. But I must repeat that it was mostly a very good life. The main concern was always my dad's health, but he went on and lived a good life until he passed away in 1960, a victim of the insidious disease that had plagued him all those years. He was but sixty years of age. Mother left us at age fifty-one, after contracting lung cancer.

We kids left Willcox. I left the summer after I returned from the service, never again to call Willcox home until I returned in 1960 to take care of Dad's affairs when he became ill and to finally take care of his estate. I was there just about two years — a whole new "ball game." Willcox had grown up. More people called the little town home, and the disadvantages of growth caught up with it and the valley. I must admit that I came back under a whole different set of circumstances. I knew I would never make Willcox my home, simply because there just wasn't anything there for me and my own family. And the whole complexion of the valley had changed. Before, it had been a true cowtown, but now there were huge farms all through the Kansas Settlement and north into the Stewart District, and many more farms were being developed. All of this was converting the once wide-open range lands. There was a different feeling and a different set of rules.

I cannot condemn too much, but I did have a keen sense of disappointment in what I saw. The old-timers who were left had gotten caught up in the boom and had gotten cynical as they saw people coming in who were not necessarily the good and honest types they had been used to dealing with. To put it simply, Willcox had joined the materialistic and affluent society. And that sure wasn't good. An indication of what had happened and was happening was the exodus of many of the old-timers themselves. They sold their businesses or they took retirement and went elsewhere. Yes, many of us return from time to time to visit the few who are left and to reminisce a bit, but not to stay.

Would I live in Willcox again? Yes, I could. A few of my friends remain, but very few, and the town is now a metropolis of some 2800 people, a far cry from our few in the thirties. The main problem would be to find gainful employment. Willcox is now an agribusiness town, living mainly off the farmer rather than the cowman. There is very little industry.

But when I say this and decry the events that have taken place in Willcox, there's still the valley and the mountains. The valley, with its patchwork quilt farmland, is changed from that standpoint, but the mountains are still the same, beautiful and wild as ever. The Chiricahuas are now designated as a wilderness area. The Galiuros are about to be, and other mountain areas might as well be, they're that inaccessible.

Many of the old-time ranches are gone now, broken up into smaller pieces or fallen victim to subdivisions, especially since the cattle market has been on the verge of complete disaster for years.

You're saying, "This guy is a character out of the past, criticizing the farmer ("sodbuster" in the early days) and promoting the rancher." Far from it. It was my dad who was the prime mover in getting the farming begun in the valley as it is today. And in many ways, I am a "frustrated" farmer, and, yes, a rancher. (Many ranchers in the Willcox area have gone into farming to grow feed and to supplement their income.)

No, I certainly do not put down the farmer. I just have hated to see the big spreads disappear. It is and has been a great way of life, which I cannot envision this country without. One of the main factors in the decline of the ranches is that the "great intellects" in Washington have seen fit to import beef, making it increasingly difficult for the rancher to keep his business. One very important fact must be brought out, and this is a major factor in keeping my sympathies with the cattle people. They have never accepted any subsidies or help from the government. Practically all other agriculture endeavors do accept this help. The rancher, even in the face of disaster and wipeout, has steadfastly refused. Ranchers have always been rugged individualists, and they will remain so. They are well aware that, should they succumb to this, they will no longer rule their own destiny. This I will always admire.

A very close friend of mine and well-known doctor of the area said it this way: "I am a staunch admirer of the cattleman. Who else but this breed of man would have had the guts to come into a wilderness area, fight the elements, stand off the Indian — and, today, live in virtual isolation, working hours that stagger the imagination." He was right. From my visits with these people I can well remember the distances between ranches, the loneliness that affected the women-folk, mostly, and yet the pride they had in their ranches, their herds, and their families. The television and movie people have gotten across that part to the public. The cowmen who I knew stood on their own two feet and let the devil take the hindmost. Today they are basically still the same. They may have bent a little in some of their endeavors, but they're still in there "pitching" to keep what is theirs and opposing any type of intervention that might interfere in their independence. I will always admire this type of man or woman!

Epilogue

We all tend to reflect on the days we grew up, and these were the golden days to most all of us. We glamorize this in our life, soon forgetting the bad times and the rough times, and our critics might say that we attempt to live in the past. This is never more true than it is today. Our society becomes more and more complicated with problems that seem to have no solution. We are beset on all sides with crime, inflation, more and more government takeover, threats of war, tension around the world. In everyday living we are faced with problems just as insurmountable. Family life no longer exists as it did in the days I have talked about. Churches have more people in them, in some cases, but less dedication. We have continued to lower our standards in everything to the point that our social, educational, and political institutions are a farce. We developed the computer to solve all these problems, and it was to be the great panacea for all. We put all our eggs in one basket — technology. But this won't do it. People are the main ingredient, and we have not maintained and developed the social and moral values of the people to go along with the technology. And so we look back at the simple and uncomplicated life we remember as young people.

Well, again, I am certainly not going back to living with kerosene lanterns or without a lot of the comforts and conveniences that we enjoy today, but I do maintain, loudly and at length, that we as a society of so-called civilized people, supposedly interested in preserving our way of life in this great country, are going to have to get off our dead ends, face the facts, and get back to the basics.

What do I mean by the "basics"? Well, here goes, and let the chips fall where they may. Time has about run out for us, for all practical purposes, to preserve our democratic way of life and to develop people who are capable and willing to meet our problems head-on. People are going to have to develop consideration for their fellowman. People are going to have to be interested and concerned about the issues that have to be solved. People are going to have to be willing to take care of themselves — to quit depending on someone else to take care of them. Ranchers and early farmers did for themselves, and they survived. People are going to have to rise up and demand leadership in their towns, their school boards, their counties, their states, and in the federal government. We do not have leadership in any form anymore. We have mealy-mouthed, self-serving politicians who don't have the guts to stand up for what is right. People can change all this. People can and will have to become involved in what goes on in their social and educational institutions. People say that they are only one vote or that they have no influence. If our pioneers who saw the valley for what it could become had felt that way, we would never have seen the development of rural power, of the farm-lands, of new feeding and range methods on the ranch, and of the industry that came to the valley (not a lot, but some did), mainly mining and power generation. People are going to have to demand and get quality education for their children;

they are going to have to make sacrifices: sacrifices in time, money, and sacrifices to serve wherever and whenever they can to achieve these things.

Do I believe that the simple solutions can prevail? *You had better believe it!* All I hear today is that the solutions to our problems are the complicated and extensive ones. Well, they don't work and they haven't worked, but I can well remember that the people I knew in my growing-up days approached their problems with directness, boldness and right-to-the-point methods. They got the job done.

There are many people who will argue this point, but I hold steadfastly that the only way to approach problems is to understand them and then meet them head-on. Sadly, we do not do this anymore. One of the biggest disappointments of my life is to return to Arizona and see the lack of leadership that has prevailed for many years in the state. We have raised a whole series of generations who cannot think for themselves, were never taught to and never tried to.

Well, so much for the sermonizing, but you can see that I do not like what I see back in the valley, specifically, and in the state and nation, generally. As I warned previously, our age-old truths, tried and tested methods, and good old-fashioned integrity have gone down the drain. We have lost the lifestyle so precious to the sustenance of the good life, and it's tragic!

There's no way that anyone will ever convince me that the youngsters today in Willcox and elsewhere are growing up with the zest for life nor the fun that we had. Life seems to have become, for many of them, a real "drag"! Well, our work is cut out for us!

I do hope that I have been able to convey, in some small way, the wonderful and fascinating life that existed in the valley, not only in my time, but in the years before that, that were the history of the valley. The memories are to be savored and preserved. Those people, from all walks of life, whether the good solid citizen or the unsavory characters that inhabited the area from time to time, were the ingredients that made up the unique atmosphere of the valley.

Sulphur Springs Valley provides the history buff with a wealth of information peculiar to only this area. And the nature lover can find a beauty there that is found nowhere else in the world.

My life there was also very different and very exciting, and, I feel, very very different from your average hometown experience.

My gratitude has to be emphasized and expressed to all those people who gave me that exciting life and, again, I can only thank the good Lord for seeing to it that I was born to Elma and Mark Bliss, my parents.